WAKE UP AMERICA

Eric Bolling

WAKE UP AMERICA

THE NINE VIRTUES THAT MADE OUR NATION GREAT—AND WHY WE NEED THEM MORE THAN EVER

ST. MARTIN'S PRESS ✠ NEW YORK

www.stmartins.com

Library of Congress Cataloging-in-Publication Data

Names: Bolling, Eric, author.
Title: Wake up America : the nine virtues that made our nation great—and why we need them more than ever / Eric Bolling.
Description: First edition. | New York, N.Y. : St. Martin's Press, 2016. | Includes bibliographical references and index.
Identifiers: LCCN 2016016562| ISBN 9781250112507 (hardcover) | ISBN 9781250121905 (signed edition) | ISBN 9781250112521 (e-book)
Subjects: LCSH: National characteristics, American. | Conservatism—United States—History. | Right and left (Political science)
Classification: LCC E169.1 .B6835 2016 | DDC 320.5—dc23
LC record available at https://lccn.loc.gov/2016016562

Our books may be purchased in bulk for promotional, educational, or business use. Please contact your local bookseller or the Macmillan Corporate and Premium Sales Department at 1-800-221-7945, extension 5442, or by e-mail at MacmillanSpecialMarkets@macmillan.com.

First Edition: June 2016

10 9 8 7 6 5 4 3 2 1

I dedicate this book to President Barack Obama.

If it weren't for your announced goal of "fundamentally transforming the United States of America," I wouldn't have been so exceedingly motivated to write this book to stop you and your liberal pals from achieving that goal.

America will survive your agenda.

CONTENTS

ACKNOWLEDGMENTS

Adrienne. For always being by my side and supporting me in all of my endeavors. I'm the luckiest man in the world to be married to you. You're my soul mate and I love you.

Eric Chase. For growing up to be an inquisitive, charitable, and ambitious young man. The world is your oyster, you'll do great and I'm extremely proud of you.

My niece—Tina Rosales—and the kids. Tina has the most amazing heart of any human being. She has two biological children, and adopted five others—all as a single mom. Tina, you're my hero. Amazing.

Roger Ailes. For taking me under his wing almost a decade ago. It's my good fortune to have the smartest, most influential man in television and news as a mentor. In *Wake Up America,* I've outlined the virtues that this country needs to get back to, and Roger's life mirrors those virtues. I'm proud to call Roger Ailes my boss and my friend.

Bill Shine. For being outstanding. Aside from Roger Ailes, Bill is the most capable television executive I've worked with. He handles more in a day than most executives will deal with in a year. Bill, I appreciate your taking an interest in my career throughout the years here at Fox. Again, a boss and a friend, Bill Shine is both.

Dianne Brandi. For being a true friend who always has great advice. You've always been there for me.

Suzanne Scott. For having an open door policy and always helping me get to the next level.

Mark Fisher. For being my friend, my business mentor, and my son's Jewish godfather. You've been a lifelong and loyal supporter. Thank you.

Sergio Gor. My former producer who continues to provide invaluable help on a daily basis and has become a true friend.

Kimberly Guilfoyle. My loyal sidekick on *The Five* who is always there when needed. I can't imagine being on *The Five* without you.

Bill O'Reilly. Filling in for the most successful man in news is a tall order. I never wavered or feared that responsibility. I always appreciated the shot. I respect Bill, the show, and the producers immensely as you can see. And that chemistry is almost impossible to re-create.

David Tabacoff, Amy Sohnen, Nate Fredman, and all *The O'Relly Factor* producers. You are the most talented group of producers in television. You have a vision and don't waver. That confidence in what they are doing exudes and the show blooms on a nightly basis.

Sean Hannity. One of the first to offer advice to me. I appreciate your always outstretched hand. Thank you.

Andrea Tantaros. You've been a rock-solid friend since day one.

To *The Five* crew of producers. You are the hardest-working group of producers I know! Thank you for that!

To my loyal *Cashin' In* producers. For giving birth to *Wake Up America,* and continuing to fight for our values every Saturday morning.

Mark Levin. For being a conservative compass, which has helped point me to becoming an advocate for smaller government. You're a legend and I value your friendship.

Glenn Beck. For giving me a chance when you hosted one of the most watched programs on TV. My first big hosting gig. I was never nervous, but I admit it was a surreal experience. You continue to be a loyal friend.

Jen Starobin. My first producer at CNBC. Jen continues to

provide advice and counsel. I wouldn't be here today without your help in the first days of my TV career.

George Witte. For taking a chance on my first book. You're a visionary and I hope to work with you and the entire team for many years to come. Your support has been unwavering.

Keith Urbahn, Matt Latimer, and Dylan Colligan of team Javelin. Your dedication in putting this book together is un-matched and *Wake Up America* would not have been possible without you. Thank you.

Kyle Nolan. My trusty aide, who is always around when some-thing needs to be fixed. Your dedication is proof you will be an outstanding journalist.

To the millions of patriotic and liberty-loving Americans (ViewCrew) who have tuned in to one of my programs, have engaged with me on Facebook and Twitter, and have now bought this book. You are the reason for my continued dedication to waking up America. Thank *you* from the bottom of my heart for all the support!

WAKE UP AMERICA

INTRODUCTION

January 20, 2017.

Inauguration Day.

A very cold day in America.

It's late January, so naturally there will be a chill in the air. The wind will whip through the crowds gathered in front of the U.S. Capitol building. However, the throngs gathered for this historic occasion will not be bothered by the cold. The true faithful wouldn't miss this for the world. They've waited for this day for a long time. They've marched, they've chanted, they've occupied, from college campuses to urban centers, just to make this possible. Today, the foot soldiers of the American Leftist movement will gain their triumph. Today, Hillary Rodham Clinton will take the oath of office as the forty-fifth President of the United States.

On the stage with Clinton are the cast of characters who will make up her administration. There's her husband, former President Bill Clinton—welfare reformer and signer of the Defense of Marriage Act, he's easily the most conservative person on the platform. All he can think about, of course, is getting back into the White House, his old stomping grounds. He tries to remember if the interns start arriving on Day One. He hopes so. The sooner the better. His role in this administration will be mostly ceremonial—a few speeches here and there, a charm offensive ready for deployment when needed. He'll have few official duties, and plenty of time for his own extracurricular activities.

Seated nearby is another familiar face: Al Gore. Once Bill

Clinton's Vice President, he's returning now as Secretary of Energy. The man who made a career out of scolding Americans for their use of evil fossil fuels—while keeping his motorcade idling outside during his speeches—will finally be able to make his environmentalist dreams into reality.

Another Al isn't far away: Al Sharpton, longtime activist for "social justice" and failed MSNBC TV host. The American public never quite caught on to the Reverend Al's unique blend of shameless self-promotion and race-baiting on MSNBC—his ratings were always terrible—but his politics line up nicely with the new President's, and he was a loyal mouthpiece on the campaign trail. So, he has been rewarded with the post of Secretary of Education. And his job is about to get a lot bigger.

Also on the stage is a man whose presence at this occasion would have seemed unthinkable six months ago—but that's politics. He is former Vermont Senator Bernie Sanders, the committed "Democratic socialist" who ended up giving Hillary Clinton a run for her money in the Democrat primary. Despite being in his seventies—only a few years older than the new President—Sanders is revered by many as the fresh face of a resurgent American brand of socialism, which was firmly embraced by the new commander in chief in her drive to win at all costs. Officially, Sanders's role in the new administration will be fixing "income inequality"—by any means necessary. However, the well-known friend to socialists around the world—who took his wife to the former Soviet Union for their honeymoon—is expected to advise Clinton on foreign policy matters as well, especially on how the United States can integrate more fully into worldwide collectivist movements.

President Hillary Clinton's inaugural address will be a rousing one. As the masses listen below and watch on televisions around the globe, she will spell out her agenda for America's long march into the twenty-first century. She will not speak of American leadership on the world stage—not even "leading from behind" as President Obama put it—but of simple "participation" in world affairs. We will end war, she proclaims to thundering cheers, by taking America out of the business of shaping the world's destiny. After all, the new President will remind us, what right have we to tell other countries what to do when our own situation is so flawed? Ironically, in years past it was Hillary Clinton who led President Obama to topple secular dictators in the Middle East in favor of radical Islamic leadership.

She will then proceed to remind us of all the social ills that plague our fellow Americans—poverty, homelessness, stagnant wages, inflating health-care costs. She will waste no time in pointing out that these are all the fault of the greedy, heartless corporations that have controlled business and politics in this country for far too long. In another carefully delivered applause line, President Clinton will remind her audience that she is in office now in order to make sure the evil corporations *pay* for what they've done—in every sense of the word.

She promises the audience at her inauguration a brand-new era—an era without uncertainty, an era without risk, an era of absolute fairness and equity. The gap between rich and poor in America will no longer be bridged, she says, but the two sides of the canyon will be shoved back together. The seas will be un-parted. No American will be left wondering why their neighbor seems to have more than they do.

The crowd hangs on her every word, and cheers for every promise. This made all the "safe space" demonstrations and Occupy protests worth it. This is what they'd been fighting for. This is what generations of Leftists before them had been fighting for. President Hillary Clinton has shown them the mountaintop—but what does the path to the summit of social-ism look like?

TWO MONTHS LATER

Two months after the inauguration, we start to see our first glimpses down that path. College students, back from their winter break and the exhilaration of the inaugural ceremonies, notice that things are a bit different on campus in the new Clinton era. College activists were the vanguard of the Clinton campaign army. While many campuses were divided between Hillary and Bernie Sanders in the primary, the #FeelTheBern crowd was soon won over once Clinton clinched the nomination and vowed to embrace her onetime competitor's unapologetic brand of "Democratic Socialism."

The Clinton team has rewarded their collegiate foot soldiers with some changes for which they have long clamored. One of the first acts of Al Sharpton's Department of Education, which has dramatically increased its involvement with higher education institutions, is that "safe space" doctrines are now required on all American college campuses. Any speech that has the slightest possibility to offend another person is confined to certain "Free Speech Zones" in public areas or during certain programs. Speaking your mind outside of these areas will be classified as a "microaggression" and result in disciplinary action from the school and referral for prosecution in a court of law. This goes for students and professors alike, and anybody on campus can be brought up in front of student-run tribunals on charges of violating the "safe space" of another individual or of the university in general.

The goal is clear: to remake the American system of higher education into a breeding ground for future guardians of political correctness. It's no longer about learning, about challenging yourself to think. No longer are American students expected (or encouraged) to live up to F. Scott Fitzgerald's definition of intelligence—"the ability to hold two opposing ideas in mind at the same time and still retain the ability to function." There's only room for one set of ideas in the American mind now—the politically correct ones. And there's no room for F. Scott Fitzgerald, either, for that matter. All he did was write about rich people.

This new American education will start even earlier than college. In the public schools, from kindergarten classrooms on up, the United Nations flag is now placed side by side with that of the United States. There is no more Pledge of Allegiance. Not only is it deemed exclusionary to the increasing number of kids born elsewhere, but it sends the wrong message. American children should now think of themselves first and foremost as "citizens of the world," and as Americans second.

Even those in the older generations, well out of school, will have no problem getting access to the "right" information. More accurately, they won't have a choice. In just the first few months of the Clinton administration, the American news media has already undergone a dramatic transformation. During the campaign, it was clear that every major news outlet—with some exceptions of center-right media—were unabashedly in the tank for Clinton. They weren't just drinking the Kool-Aid, they were swimming in it.

After her election, it was decided that her cheerleading networks should simply drop their whole "impartial" act entirely. Why continue the charade of denying the reality of their bias when they can just join the May Day Parade already? In the interest of "fairness" and "progress," mainstream media organizations consolidate themselves in a series of mergers, initiated and overseen by the government. The government then takes over the combined entities to create a single state propaganda mouthpiece, under the now greatly expanded authority of the Federal Communications Commission.

This takes so much guesswork out of the equation for consumers. This way, they won't have to worry about conflicting perspectives. They can go to one place for all the news their benevolent Uncle Sam (or Aunt Hillary) deems fit to print. All the information is handpicked, vetted, and curated to suit the needs of the people—and their government.

Whose perspectives *do* get airtime under the new regime? Since all legal media is now effectively government media, many of the new "media personalities" are in fact government officials.

Some high-profile members of the Cabinet host their own shows. Bernie Sanders gives "inspiring" lectures on the evils of pay gaps every Saturday and Sunday—*Weekends with Bernie,* they call the series. Al Gore's 2006 environmental horror flick *An Inconvenient Truth* is shown frequently, with new commentary and interviews with the Secretary of Energy himself included to bring modern viewers up to date. Most kids will have seen the original—it will be required viewing in schools.

Schoolchildren, too, will be treated to frequent addresses by Education Secretary Sharpton, who also is back on afternoon television with educational shows that are *strongly recommended* for after-school viewing. Sometimes the Reverend Secretary will bring in special guests, like Professor (and former domestic terrorist) Bill Ayers to present his special *10-Part History of the United States.* Grab the kids—it's "edutainment" for the whole family!

Not only will everyone hear more from government officials, but we will hear more from the President herself. Between traditional media, which has now gone completely over to her side, and social media—where the White House bully pulpit carries a lot of weight among followers—we hear something from or about President Hillary Clinton every single day, on multiple occasions.

There's a calculated reason for this constant intrusion. Team Clinton wants us to get used to hearing from them as much as possible. Soon, Hillary and her advisers will be more than just government officials making pronouncements. They'll become trusted friends, and whatever message they're spouting will be immediately accepted by viewers. More than that, consumers will welcome the idea of people from the government frequently beaming into their lives to discuss some matter of no doubt vital national importance. That makes eventual government involvement, and further government control, therefore seem necessary.

One of the many uses for a propaganda apparatus is the

fomentation of crisis. And as veteran Leftist operative Rahm Emanuel said, "Never let a crisis go to waste." Early in her administration, President Hillary Clinton invents a crisis in order to achieve a longtime liberal policy goal. She declares that gun violence is a national emergency that threatens us all, and sets the Department of Homeland Security to the task of confiscating all firearms from law-abiding Americans until the "problem" is solved. The National Rifle Association is deemed a hate-mongering organization, and their Virginia headquarters is raided by federal agents. Yet the government is careful to point out that this is not a permanent "gun grab." Citizens deemed trustworthy and obedient by the federal government may be able to get their guns back once the government determines the "crisis" is over, which will be sometime between now and never.

With the guns out of the way, the process of radical wealth redistribution begins. President Clinton made sure in her inaugural address to remind American entrepreneurs that they didn't achieve hard-earned success on their own, and her Treasury Secretary, Bernie Sanders, soon tells them it's time to spread the wealth around. A national minimum wage hike is put into effect, with no recourse for the small businesses forced to close by the new policy. Even entrepreneurs' personal property is not safe; it's been deemed that some of them have "too much." That vacation home you spent your whole life working and saving for? You don't need that—time to turn it over to the state.

The federal government may also come after your car, but for a different reason. Energy Secretary Gore's department has been given sweeping new powers, and he's tossing vehicles off the road left and right. The SUV that you load up to take your kids to soccer practice? It's been outlawed by the Environmental Protection Agency. You'll be provided with a voucher to exchange it for a hybrid, a cash rebate for a bicycle, or coupons to use on public transportation—your choice.

When none of these initiatives seem to be solving the unemployment crisis in America—and are even starting to make it worse—President Clinton turns to a solution that is as simple as it is elegant. It addresses the most glaring problem with one of the Left's pet issues: political correctness. Unemployed Millennials and former Occupy activists—the people who got Clinton elected—are put to work under a new Homeland Security program designed to police hate speech. Any language deemed to be racist, sexist, or seen to promote inequality, patriarchy, and white privilege will now be punishable under the law. Citizens are encouraged to report any conversations or symbols that might trigger them. Power to decide what constitutes hate speech is delegated to a rotating council of Left-wing academics appointed by the President, and their powers are enforced by the roving gangs of activist thugs who were until recently unemployed. Their zeal for political correctness is such that it makes Mao's Red Guard look like a church youth group.

When these gangs start raiding the homes and businesses of anyone they think has offended someone else, when non-regime-approved journalists are forced to broadcast in secret, when personal property is simply confiscated for violating new rules, people will start to look around at some point and start to wonder where it all began. It began on Inauguration Day, 2017, a cold day for America—when the chill in the air was nothing compared to the chilling effect on our freedom brought about by the rise of socialism.

These aren't concrete predictions. Instead, let's think of them as hypotheticals. The specifics of the scenario don't even matter that much. It doesn't matter whether the President of the United States is Hillary Clinton or Bernie Sanders or Joe Biden or Mickey Mouse—as long as it's someone who pushes a progressive, radical Leftist ideology, we are in danger. Radical Leftist attitudes have taken hold across many different facets of our culture, with the goal of forcing America steadily toward European-style socialism. This book aims to help wake us up to that threat. I still hope and pray that if we wake up in time, we may be able to avoid anything like the grim future I've just imagined.

Forced conformity, redistribution of wealth, a preoccupation with "fairness." Does any of that sound familiar? Lots of books have been written and many movies made about societies that try to create a utopia and end up simply enslaving their people. George Orwell's *1984* springs to mind pretty quickly. Yet there's one classic example by the American author Kurt Vonnegut, which tears the whole false notion of utopia open in a concise, tight narrative. It's a short story called "Harrison Bergeron," first published in 1961.

"Harrison Bergeron" shows us what's at stake when a society gets too preoccupied with fairness, when success becomes vilified. By the end of the story, it's clear that most of the people in this society have lost most of their basic humanity. In the face of unspeakable tragedy, they just go on about their lives, so beaten down and "handicapped" that they cannot register or process simple human emotions. They are no longer conscious of what it means to truly be alive. All because their society— their government—would rather everyone be equal and soulless than some do better in life than others.

"Harrison Bergeron" is fiction, obviously. It was written, though, at a time when the shadow of communism was spread over large swaths of the world. It can be taken as the warning of a writer—a very eccentric and individualistic one at that— about the dangers of state-enforced egalitarianism that was so rampant in the collectivist societies of the time. And it's no less relevant today.

The America we live in does not resemble the America I grew up in. Back then, we all recognized the beauty of the American dream, the radical notion that the embracing of hard work and traditional values was the path to prosperity and social mobility. Today many scoff at that notion. Socialism is cool now. Cool enough to allow a tome defending socialism—Thomas Piketty's

Capital in the Twenty-First Century—to become one of the most popular books of our time. It's unclear when this backward ideology made a comeback, but in 2008, a Democrat from the academic socialist circles of Chicago, Barack Obama, won the election on a promise of "fundamentally transforming the United States of America."[1] Obama's platform promised the use of cooperative radical changes that would fundamentally transform America, and it struck a chord with young people desperate for answers in a bad economy.

Three years later, raggedy, disheveled Millennials in bandannas and Che Guevara T-shirts took to the streets in America's cities. From Manhattan's Zuccotti Park to Oakland's Ogawa Plaza they "occupied," demanding free health care, free college, and freedom from personal hygiene and personal responsibility. While these modern-day flower children didn't have any specific legislative goals, their demands were clear: a radical redistribution of wealth and reorganization of society. They demanded an America where the state used any means necessary to achieve equality.

We've seen radical experiments in equality before. For most of the twentieth century, members of both parties stood strong against the threat of Soviet and Chinese communism—both radical experiments in socialism. Men like John F. Kennedy and Ronald Reagan made the case for American exceptionalism and called the Soviet Union what it was: an "Evil Empire." It was through the determined efforts of men like that, and the superiority of the American system that we ultimately won the Cold War. In 1989, the Berlin Wall that separated East Germany from West Germany, and the free world from the Iron Curtain of Soviet communism, came tumbling down. Ronald Reagan famously told his Soviet counterpart Mikhail Gorbachev to "tear down this wall!" but before he could, Germans did, using anything they could find, including their bare hands. When the Berlin Wall fell, Soviet communism came down with it.

Nation after nation declared independence from the Soviet

Union, and for the first time, the world truly saw the stark contrast between the free world and the totalitarian misery of the Eastern bloc. The West was dominated by skyscrapers, shopping malls, and supermarkets stocked with five of everything; the egalitarian East? It was dominated by dreary ghetto-style block housing, bread lines, and censorship. The contrast was clear. This should have been the end of socialism. It should have been consigned to the dustbin of history.

But it wasn't. As time moved on, the prosperity America afforded us allowed us to forget about the prisons, the bread lines, and the secret police. We forgot about Solzhenitsyn's tales of Siberian gulags and Stalinist oppression. The idea of something for nothing was apparently so appealing that we let slick politicians explain to us that socialism wasn't so bad, that it was more Sweden than Stalingrad. Apparently, it worked. That's perhaps the only explanation for an America where a Woodstock-era socialist Senator from Vermont who honeymooned in the Soviet Union during its darkest days was able to speak to packed crowds of young people across the country. It's not just the kids, though. People who should know better are utterly clueless. When pressed on the difference between a Democrat and a socialist by MSNBC host Chris Matthews, Democratic National Committee Chair Debbie Wasserman Schultz couldn't come up with an answer.[2] In defending his film *Trumbo,* which casts communist Hollywood collaborators in a sympathetic light, celebrated *Breaking Bad* star Bryan Cranston attempted to apologize for Soviet communism by incorrectly stating that reviled dictator Joseph Stalin wasn't actually a communist, but a fascist (as if he'd know the difference).[3] It's no wonder that a majority of young Americans polled today say they prefer to elect a "socialist" over a "capitalist."

America's elite universities were once fertile ground for debate where students discussed ideas that were both classical and experimental, traditional and controversial. Students demanded the right to free speech. A generation later, students are demanding freedom *from* speech. Now, college campuses are places where coddled Millennials go to get indoctrinated by 1960s radicals. Ten years ago we worried about liberal bias on college campuses, but today students are demanding it, calling for protection from conversations and symbolism that they deem "triggering," a catchall term for anything anyone anywhere might find mildly offensive. Censorship has long been a tool used by the politically powerful to stamp out dissent and stifle protest—yet today's kids, ignorant of the past, are demanding it!

There's simply no mistaking it: American values are under attack. We face real threats from abroad, but there's a more subtle danger that we often overlook: the collapse of the virtues that helped make this country great. They are precisely the pillars of our society that the Left knows they have to undermine in order to create their bleak, gray, egalitarian utopia. I know them well, not just because they've saved my country since its founding, they've also saved me. I was a kid who came from nothing, took some risks, and made a good life for myself and my family in a way that could only happen in America.

President Ronald Reagan famously said that "freedom is never more than one generation away from extinction."

But after President Ronald Reagan won the Cold War, the socialist threat is arguably more subversive. In their endeavor to radically reform American society, the socialist Left has used fear, shame, and class warfare to divide us. They recognize that doing so is essential to destroying the many qualities that have made America an exceptional nation since its founding. Those nine core values—grit, profit, manliness, thrift, individuality, dominion, merit, pride, and providence—are qualities that defined my experience in America and many others. They were essential to my own personal success, and restoring their primacy is key to restoring the American dream. Now is the time to wake up America.

1. GRIT

noun \'grit

(1.) mental toughness and courage
—Merriam-Webster's definition

(1.) an archaic descriptor denoting male-chauvinist microaggression in the form of an oppressive, traditionalist/individualist approach to adversity

(2.) a hardness of character that renders individuals unsuitable members of a progressive, collectivist society
—A Leftist's definition

If your determination is fixed, I do not counsel you to despair. Few things are impossible to diligence and skill. Great works are performed not by strength, but perseverance.

—SAMUEL JOHNSON

I hate the question, "What's the secret of your success?" There is no secret to being successful. Ask anybody who is successful and they will say some version of the same thing—perseverance, mental toughness, or my personal favorite: grit.

Grit is getting up again and again after being knocked down to continue the fight. Grit is going over, around, or straight through obstacles to reach your goals—no matter how much it hurts to do so. Grit is the power to try, fail, and rebuild yourself in a nation of endless possibilities. Grit is the soul of the American spirit.

But in our society, we value grit less every day. Thanks to radical Leftists, the liberal media, and collectivist stalwarts teaching our kids at all educational levels, "grit" is no longer considered an essential component of success—or of the American character. We value our personal security and our personal liberty, but they're not the same thing. Sometimes, the freedoms we enjoy under personal liberty can shake the foundations of our personal security.

Here's the thing: to be gritty and tough, you have to take risks, and by definition with risk comes the possibility of failure—a lack of security. The grit comes in when you fail, get back up, dust yourself off, and keep trying, as many times as it takes for you to get the job done. That's why grit is such an essential component of the American character. We've always been a mentally tough people—because we had to be. You can't survive slavery or brave weeks on a rickety ship on the Atlantic without some serious grit, folks.

Grit, however, is anathema to liberals. Gritty, free-thinking citizens are harder to control. Oh, sure, liberals love to spout happy talk about perseverance and the American Dream, but they are doing everything they can to make sure there is only one path to this dream: through the government. What they don't realize is that if the government is the way, it actually *isn't* the American Dream anymore. Because the American Dream is about building something for yourself, not about being handed something by someone else, especially not a bloated, inefficient, deck-stacking government.

Liberals, by nature, just aren't comfortable with risk. The dirty little secret of liberalism is that, at least in today's form, it's not liberal at all. Liberals don't want "liberty." They can't handle the messiness of real democracy in a dynamic republic. Instead of allowing individual citizens to pave their own way in life, liberals want a bunch of technocratic "experts" to decide what is best for the rest of us.

So, it is very much in the Left's interests for the citizenry to be soft, docile, and obedient. That's why liberals have spent decades putting forth what I sometimes call the "softness doctrine," which tells Americans that the ideal person is conformist, collectivist, and in need of government assistance in nearly every aspect of life. Think of the 2012 Obama campaign's "Life of Julia" nonsense as the perfect example. This slideshow tells the life story of the fictional cartoon character "Julia" and how she benefited from a benevolent government literally from cradle to grave.[1]

It's also perfect nonsense. Do you think it was an accident that the Obama team created a cartoon to tell this story? It's fitting that the tale is told in the same media form as a Disney fairy tale, because Julia's life is just as much a fantasy as Cinderella's or Snow White's. It's the Joe Camel of political advertisements.

This is how they spread the "softness doctrine." Our government, media, and academia are brainwashing all of us—especially our kids—into being mushy blobs of fragile self-esteem, all in the name of "progressivism."

As they do with masculinity itself, today's liberals treat grit like an anachronism from a time when people hadn't evolved enough to live in the progressive paradise that they believe is just around every corner. Grit is unnecessary. You don't have to be mentally tough, because if you have a problem, a supposedly benevolent government will take care of it *for* you—and take care *of* you.

While this cotton candy philosophy may make sense to sophomoric college students and sheltered media elites, those of us who have fought in the trenches of our own lives, the global economy, and the nation's politics know better. You can't save everyone, and when you try to do so, you end up doing much more harm than good.

This isn't just a social problem—though it most certainly is that—it is also an economic and national security problem. Do you think China and Russia will sit back and let us continue to be the most powerful nation in the world once we're too soft to fight for market share—or even our homeland?

As a nation, we need to toughen up, stop whining, and get to work.

PARENT TRAP

When I was a kid, I loved to ride my bike. I especially loved doing tricks like popping wheelies, skidding, flying off of make-shift ramps—the more dangerous it was, the more fun it was to do. I did it without a parent or other adult supervisor hovering over me, pretending to be a guardian angel. I'll put my faith in God's own angels, thank you very much. Getting to ride a bike was my first taste of true freedom. I could go farther, faster than ever before, and all on my own. On my bike adventures, I was my own master—taking on both the joys and responsibilities that freedom demands.

I bet a lot of folks reading this book could tell a similar story about riding bikes as kids. The speed. The fun. The *freedom* of it. Juxtapose this freedom with the bike-riding experience of children today. Swaddled in more padding and headgear than an NFL fullback, it's amazing these kids can even get on their bikes, let alone ride them. And when these little plastic-and-Velcro-encased darlings do finally get going on their two-wheelers, you bet your ass they have to stay in specific areas under tight adult supervision. We're so scared of our kids getting hurt, we barely let them out of our sight until they are in their mid- to late-teens.

This is not entirely the parents' fault. Driven by liberal col-lectivist dogma, as delivered through politicians, activists, aca-demia, and the media, we are taught that we must make our children's paths through life as easy as possible. We do every-thing we can to expose them to what we consider positive, while avoiding anything negative as if it were a nuclear waste dump full of lepers.[2]

Due to intensive liberal propaganda that has morphed into a bizarre kind of social pressure, parents have taken on "softness indoctrination" like a religion. Before a kid is even born, parents are inundated with a thousand "musts" for being a good mother or father. They "must" take the right prenatal vitamins. They "must" do the right kinds of exercises. They "must" keep calm so their baby doesn't feel any negative emotions through the umbilical cord. They "must" buy the insanely overwrought and overpriced strollers, cribs, and (especially) car seats on the market today if they want to keep their kids safe.

But the real indoctrination begins with the actual raising of a child. Quite simply, we are told to protect our children from *everything,* and if we don't, we're bad parents. The "softness indoctrination" industry preys on this very real fear that all parents have, especially new parents. It's disgusting, disingenuous, and it's a major reason why grit is being taken out of the American character.

Of course, we all want our kids to be safe, but there is a point of diminishing returns when it comes to safety. If your kids never face any real challenges or dangers when young, they will have no idea how to handle themselves when they face problems as adults. As so-called Millennials join the workforce—the first generation of the ultra-ultra-coddled to do so—we're seeing examples of just how ill-equipped these kids are to handle the rigors of the real world.

Do you think those stories of parents of Millennials calling bosses to complain about something on their adult child's behalf are urban legends? Think again. In July 2015, employee dynamics expert Lisa Orrell, CPC, wrote an entire blog post[3] about how widespread this phenomenon is. Orrell wrote:

> In my SEVEN YEARS of being a keynote speaker and conducting workshops for companies about how to better recruit, manage and retain Millennial talent, I've yet to ask this question and NOT get a hand raised: "Who here has heard from the parent of one of your Millennial employees?"

This is especially scary when you consider, as Orrell notes, that by "2025, 75% of the workforce will be Millennials." Will we have "bat phones" from all the retirement communities to all the corporate headquarters in America by then? What the hell are we going to do when these perpetual children are in charge?

As our children age, the "softness indoctrination" continues in school and in sports, and intensifies into a cult of self-esteem: It values self-esteem above all qualities while also taking away the tools for fostering and maintaining it. Today, everybody gets a trophy. We're so afraid of hurting someone's feelings, we deceive our children into thinking collaboration always trumps competition, and that there are no losers in the game of life.

That is why college campuses today require so-called safe spaces for students who feel overwhelmed by . . . whatever it is they feel overwhelmed by. It's also why anything that an overly sensitive student finds objectionable—especially in the context of race, ethnicity, gender, or sexual orientation—is called a "microaggression." We're getting to the point where the very sight of a straight, white male is an affront. They even have a term for us average folks: "cis"—as in "cisgender." I'm not sure whether we're supposed to think being "cis" a good thing or a bad thing.

But what else do we expect from an educational system that subverts competition, champions unrealistic levels of collaboration, and neuters male behavior in a constant effort to "feminize" boys and men? We can't be surprised our children are bizarrely fragile—it's what we've been taught to teach them, and what they've been taught, for decades.

All of this combines to create an intense, even crippling, fear of failure in Millennials. And people who are terrified of failure are much less likely to take the kinds of risks that are necessary to grow an economy, build character, and sustain and continue to improve upon a great nation.

TRY, TRY AGAIN

I played baseball in high school and college, and was drafted by the Pittsburgh Pirates to play in their minor league system, but after a shoulder injury ended my baseball dream, I was lost. I went back to Chicago, where I had grown up and my parents lived, to figure out my life. I was broke and needed a job. And I didn't want to be some cipher on the welfare rolls, though that would have been the easiest thing to do.

So you know what my dad did? He didn't have a good cry with me and tell me it was okay to wallow in my own self-pity. Instead, he dropped the classified section of the newspaper on the table with a Mobil Oil ad circled.

The cattle-call job interview was being held at the O'Hare Hyatt, and when the day arrived, I thought I was in luck. A massive snowstorm was pummeling Chicago—typical winter—and I figured most folks would be stuck inside, unable or unwilling to make the trek out to the airport. Maybe, I thought, if I was really lucky I'd be the only guy there!

Boy, was I wrong. When I arrived, there were hundreds at the Hyatt who had braved the weather for a shot at this job. The line wrapped out the door and down the hallway. I waited my turn—patient, but hungry.

When I met with the Mobil executives doing the interview, they had one question. One of the execs held up a Bic pen and said simply, "Sell this to me."

I was stunned for a second. I could see my job prospects evaporating before my eyes. I felt a cold sweat break out and start to trickle down my back. Instead of panicking, though, I cleared my mind for a second—then it hit me. I knew what to do.

I said, "Okay, I'll sell this pen to you. It's a great pen, it lasts a long time, and it's very good for the price, which is fifty cents." Then I added, "But I'll do you one better. I'll sell you three pens for a dollar."

I saw the Mobil guys look at one another and smile. In that instant, I knew I got the job. It was like the great ballgame I played in college that I knew would get me drafted into the pros. Sometimes, you just know.

Of course, at the time, I wasn't sure why *exactly* they picked me and a handful of others. Six of us were hired out of hundreds of applicants who showed up in the middle of a snowstorm. It was only after beginning the Mobil training program that I realized why I was hired. Mobil is a gasoline producer and marketer. They make more money as their number of gallons sold increases. In other words, they rely on beating down prices to sell more overall gas, just as I had cut down the price of a pen to sell more of them.

I didn't have a clue about any of this at the time, but I learned the basics of how commodities work—and in commodities I would make my name, and my fortune. Sometimes it's better to be lucky than good. Even more than that, it's better to be motivated—to have the grit and determination it takes to keep going even after a major failure or challenge. That's what lets you risk crushing disappointment for a chance at major success.

TRUE GRIT: GENERAL GEORGE WASHINGTON

The concept of grit is at the very heart of American democracy, economics, and history. The American Dream itself is an homage to grit: work hard, never give up, and you'll succeed in your endeavors, and deservedly reap the benefits. Ours is a nation hewn out of raw wilderness. We created the greatest system of government in history, twice saved the world from tyrannical domination in the world wars, and then again in the Cold War. We've faced down mighty challenges, all with our gritty, tough-minded determination.

Think about our ancestors. Almost all of us are the descendants of immigrants, whether free or involuntary. In each case, our American ancestors had to endure situations and challenges we'd find almost unbelievable today: cutting roads and farms out of virgin forest, having your spouse or children sold and never seeing them again, braving the angry Atlantic in hopes of a better life and more liberty for you, your family, and your descendants.

We are the children of risk-takers, and have strength of will and character built into our DNA. And it's just these strengths that allowed us to tame a vast wilderness, create the most powerful economy and nation ever seen on earth, and help spread freedom and justice around the world. It's been with us from the very beginning, from the first settlers and slaves up through World War II and the beginnings of the Cold War. It wasn't until the 1960s that the long slide to softness began.

The greatest example of the true power of American grit comes from the man who exemplified the word: George Washington. Though we tend to think of Washington today as a stiff, refined figure—which he was—we cannot forget that the formal face Washington put on in public was backed by an absolutely iron will and determination to see his countrymen set free of the yoke of British tyranny. One could argue that it was his sheer grit that defeated what was then one of the world's great superpowers.

Lost in the mists of nostalgia is the fact that Washington endured numerous failures before finally turning the tide of the war and bringing about its successful end at Yorktown in 1781.[4] In fact, the war itself could have been lost in the first year or two if it weren't for Washington's gritty determination. After being appointed commander in chief by the Continental Congress, Washington rushed to Boston to take over command of the ragtag band that made up the Continental Army.[5]

After successfully driving the British from Boston, however, Washington smartly figured out that the British would try to capture New York City next, so he quickly moved his men south. Washington's army was defeated, though, and forced to abandon New York, and then suffered a series of defeats as they were steadily driven into New Jersey. Finally, Washington was able to cross the Delaware River and bring his men (and himself) a brief respite.[6]

Washington was in trouble, and he knew it. He'd lost a lot of men, and those who were left were exhausted, demoralized, and in many cases ready to go home when their enlistments were up. Instead of succumbing to despair, though, Washington drew upon his heroic well of grit, rallied his men, and won a daring, crushing victory over the Hessians—German mercenaries allied with the British—in Trenton, New Jersey, on the night of Christmas 1776.[7] Taking advantage of the momentum, Washington moved on to defeat a force of British regulars at Princeton just days later.

Washington faced another tough winter the following year. After defeats at the battles of Brandywine and Germantown, the Continental Army set up their winter camp in Valley Forge, Pennsylvania, about twenty miles from Philadelphia.[8] We all know about the hardships of Valley Forge—not having enough food, clothing, or fuel for heat, our brave patriots and their tough-minded commander endured a level of physical and mental discomfort few (outside our outstanding military) could stand today.

Washington, however, didn't spend this time pouting—he got to work training his men and doing everything he could to keep up morale. He also spent enormous amounts of energy trying to get Congress to pay for more supplies and fighting off accusations of incompetence, including at least one high-level attempt to unseat him. The result? In June, a much stronger and better-trained Continental Army emerged from Valley Forge, ready to face the enemy.[9] Once again, Washington's grit—his strong will and mental fortitude—kept the army, and our country, together.

And Washington was just one of many men and women whose determination helped push the United States forward and make us a great country: from the Founding Fathers to Abraham Lincoln to Ronald Reagan, gritty, tough Americans have been the driving force in making us great. However, we've lost our way—and nowhere is this more evident than in our limping economy.

GRIT FORGES THE AMERICAN ECONOMY

For most of our nation's history, our economic policies were based on the philosophy of the father of economic "grit"—Adam Smith, whose famous *Wealth of Nations* was published the same year (1776) as the nation that would most vigorously embrace his philosophy—at least until recently—was born.

Smith wrote the book on economics—literally. *The Wealth of Nations* was the first book on economics to capture the public's interest. Why? It's no mystery. In this groundbreaking tome, Smith outlines the positive power of determined self-interest (i.e., grit) and how both drive mighty public goods. It should be required reading for every student—especially every college student, and even more especially their professors—in the United States.

In one of the book's most famous quotes, Smith states that it is "not from the benevolence of the butcher, the brewer, or the baker, that we can expect our dinner, but from their regard to their own interest."[10] Instead, people's actions—and therefore the free market as a whole—are led by what Smith famously called an "invisible hand" that promotes "an end which was no part of [one's] intention."[11]

In fact, says Smith, by pursuing one's own interest, an individual "frequently promotes [the interest] of the society more effectually than when he really intends to promote it."[12] Centuries ago, Smith recognized this essential truth, upon which the economies of much of the world are now at least partially based.

What Smith is saying is that as we successfully pursue our self-interest—which can only be done with grit and determination—we help create a stronger, better, and freer society for everyone. With a handful of exceptions, up until the 1930s, this was America's approach to economics, resulting in the rise of the United States as an economic powerhouse and geopolitical giant.

But then came the Great Depression and the election of Franklin D. Roosevelt as President. The tentative collectivist roots of Roosevelt's "New Deal" matured throughout the 1940s and 1950s, and were hardened by Lyndon Johnson's "Great Society" in the 1960s, when things began to fall apart. This collectivist—really, socialist—trend has now found its purest expression in Barack Obama's "hope and change" administration.

During this time—with the exception of the Reagan Eighties—America and Americans continued to soften. And we're now a nation of wusses. We let China walk all over us when it comes to currency manipulation. We let Russia push us around in the Middle East. And our people look more and more to government to tell them what to do, instead of taking risks, building our own lives, and creating wealth for ourselves and our communities.

To a degree, we are victims of our own success. As our country grew more powerful, and wealth and technology made life easier, a certain amount of softening was probably inevitable. Where we are today, though, is not a natural progression of a society—it is the deliberate outcome of decades of indoctrination intended to turn what used to be a nation of mavericks into a nation of sheep. We avoid risk, seek safety, and cower in corners—both real and proverbial.

And it's killing our economy, literally. Between 2012 and 2014, GDP growth was just 2 percent.[13] This is considered the "new normal" of growth, at least according to the tame liberal media, which keeps trying to convince us that this is a strong recovery. This is utter and complete bullshit. This has been the worst recovery in nearly a century,[14] as further evidenced by the "good" employment numbers we keep hearing about.

Every time new, lower unemployment numbers come out, the liberals and the media (but I repeat myself) tout how the job market has bounced back from the Great Recession. What they fail to mention is the historically low workforce participation rate.

According to a July 2015 *U.S. News & World Report* analysis, the "country's labor force participation rate—which measures the share of Americans at least 16 years old who are either employed or actively looking for work—dipped last month to a 38-year low, clocking in at an underwhelming 62.6 percent."[15] Translation: the jobs numbers look "good" not because we are creating tons of good jobs, but because so many people have given up looking for work—or simply don't want to work, because they know that Mama Government will be there to take care of them.

Anemic 2 percent GDP growth and an insanely low workforce participation rate are perfect economic metaphors and indicators of the Left's "softness doctrine." Essentially, we are being told that this economy is "good enough," and that we should accept our lot. That's not the American way, though—and that's not the conservative way, either. We can only hope the next President is a true, pro-growth conservative who will return our economy and society to its gritty, tough-as-nails roots.

CRAMER VS. CRAMER

Without great risk, we cannot achieve great success. I learned this lesson pretty clearly once when I'd just started out on television. I found myself going head-to-head with the then-biggest name in finance TV, Jim Cramer. Cramer, whose show *Mad Money* was known for its off-the-wall antics as much as its stock tips, was still regarded as the "big dog" when it came to stocks and bonds. I was relatively new to CNBC, mostly talking commodities—but I had started to branch out into general financial analysis as well.

I must have been making somewhat of a name for myself—and apparently pissing off Big Jim for some reason—because I heard through the grapevine that Cramer was on the warpath.

For me. In fact, I learned he wanted to come onto *Fast Money* where I was a panelist specifically for the purpose of taking me down a peg or two. I wasn't sure why, but I sure as hell wasn't going to back down, either.

I didn't doubt my own financial analysis, but Cramer was a TV pro, and could make almost anybody look like a fool in front of millions of viewers. I felt like I was being backed into a corner. I'd worked so hard to get where I was, to do well as a trader and then to break into TV, and now one of the biggest guns in the business was coming for me. So I went to see Mark Fisher, my mentor from the trading floor, to talk things out. Mark Fisher was a real sage. He never spelled things out for me, but he helped me figure them out for myself through sharp analysis.

We agreed that if Cramer wanted, he could come after me then and there. But then, Mark asked a simple question: What if I won? "Would Cramer risk you beating him?" Mark asked. No, I realized, he wouldn't. "Think about that for a second," Mark said. And I did.

So the day came when Cramer was due to appear on our show. He didn't go after me right away, but instead started talking about how good the stock market was looking. I saw my opening. I jumped in, cut him off, and said simply, "Cramer, you're wrong." Big Jim looked stunned. The panelists were stunned. And I'm sure the audience was stunned.

"What do you mean I'm wrong," he stammered, clearly not used to hearing that phrase. I was ready. I told him that I thought commodities were a better bet than financial stocks, and decided to make it interesting.

"I'll bet you fifty thousand dollars for charity," I offered, "and you can have your financial stocks, which don't look good to me, and I'll take gold and oil. We'll come back one year from now and we'll see who does better, and the loser pays the winner's charity fifty grand."

Cramer had no idea what to do. He couldn't back down,

though, not in the face of the upstart new guy. All he could get out was: "Big hat, no cattle, pal" and finally "on your way!"

This exchange happened just before the financial meltdown that started with the banking sector, which held all the stocks Cramer had picked. Every single stock that he talked about tanked over the next year: Lehman Brothers, Bear Stearns, all the big financials, they all went belly-up. Gold and oil, of course, rallied because investors abandoned banks to seek shelter in commodities. Gold and oil doubled, and his stocks got wiped out. And that moment is preserved on YouTube for all to see.[16]

A year passed, and I never heard anything about the bet. I haven't heard anything to this day. I took a gamble confronting a veteran financial guru on live TV, and it paid off—at least for me and my reputation. However, I can think of some deserving charities that would really appreciate that $50,000, and Cramer could certainly afford to pay it. His silence has been deafening.

I didn't set out to humiliate Jim Cramer, but I wasn't going to let him humiliate me. I had to stake out my territory, and prove I belonged in the TV big leagues just as much as he did. Mark Fisher helped me realize my opening: Cramer was afraid of losing to me. That was his weakness, and I exploited it. It was just like when I had to fight—sometimes literally—my way to the top of the trading pits. You define your objective, then figure out what (or who) is in your way. What set me apart was an intense desire to solve the problem. I made my analysis, took Mark's advice, and eventually the way opened and I was able to meet the challenge.

THE ENDGAME

The kind of risk-taking I demonstrated with Jim Cramer is a good example of the grit necessary to build and sustain a great country. It is also exactly what the Left is trying to grind down with its collectivist policies and "softness indoctrination." Instead of challenging the status quo and trusting in your own abilities, they would rather you trust in government. Just stop worrying and let the state do the thinking for you, right? Why make things hard for yourself?

After all, they know more than you do about choosing what information you get, what nonprofit groups should be allowed to function, what social services you need, and what kind of health care you deserve. Who needs grit to sustain themselves when you can just sit back and let the government take care of everything? The softer the citizenry, the more susceptible they are to liberal claptrap—and the more strings the Leftist puppet masters can pull.

And all along the way, a biased media, a morally bankrupt academy, and a clueless Hollywood have abetted this softening. Rugged manliness is denigrated—being "macho" is assumed to be the same thing as being a male chauvinist. Being a thug or an outlaw is cool, while being a soldier or police officer is a tool of oppression. And besides, crime is a result of social conditions, not personal choices. Children are taught that the world is full of dangers—which is true—and that they aren't capable of handling them without government assistance—which is a lie.

Speaking of truth and lies, on September 29, 2011, President Obama said the following:

> I mean, there are a lot of things we can do. The way I think about it is, you know, this is a great, great country that had gotten a little soft and, you know, we didn't have that same competitive edge that we needed over the last couple of decades. We need to get back on track.[17]

Hearing this, I didn't know whether to laugh, cry . . . or put my fist through a wall. This may be the truest thing this President has ever said, and yet he has done everything in his power to make us softer! This is the kind of media bait-and-switch liberals excel at. Their hypocrisy knows no bounds, and their souls know no shame. To the liberal, their ends are so obviously good (to them), that any means are justified. Think I'm wrong? Pick up a book about Stalin or Mao and you'll see that I'm 100 percent right.

However, it is important to note one thing: there are a few major exceptions to today's "softness indoctrination." The biggest and by far most important is the U.S. military. Our soldiers, sailors, airmen, and marines are among the toughest, grittiest folks to ever walk the planet. Those who have fought in Iraq, Afghanistan, and the war on terror in general—as well as many of our first responders and law enforcement—are the exception to today's soft America.

In today's America, you can choose to be soft. In the old days, you had to be prepared to be tough, even if the fight you were preparing for never came. While the full reasoning behind this softness is unknowable, there is no doubt in my mind that the policies and philosophy of the Left—including and especially Barack Obama—have played the primary role in the deterioration of our national grit, character, and mental toughness.

2. PROFIT

America's abundance was created not by public sacrifices to "the common good," but by the productive genius of free men who pursued their own personal interests and the making of their own private fortunes. They did not starve the people to pay for America's industrialization. They gave the people better jobs, higher wages, and cheaper goods with every new machine they invented, with every scientific discovery or technological advance—and thus the whole country was moving forward and profiting, not suffering, every step of the way.

—AYN RAND

The pharmaceutical industry. ExxonMobil. Bain Capital. McDonald's. Walmart. Monsanto. Goldman Sachs.

These are just a few of the giants in corporate America that have become synonymous with villainy among the political Left. Liberals from Barack Obama to Hillary Clinton—and their allies in the mainstream media—constantly attack "corporate greed" and "excessive corporate profits" while pretending they care about Middle America. To make their case, they often cite one or more of the above by name.

Predictably, the holier-than-thou elitists of Hollywood have gotten into this act—with a multitude of films or TV programs about evil CEOs (i.e., Lex Luthor, Mr. Burns, the bald guy in *Iron Man*) willing to risk the very survival of humanity for a quick buck (i.e., Jurassic Park/World, Spectre, the Terminator films). All throughout the George W. Bush administration, of course, there were any number of movies depicting the war in Iraq as a cynical attempt to grab oil and increase profits for multinational corporations (like the dreaded Halliburton).

It's even more nefarious when they go after the youngest viewers. In December 2011 *The Muppets,* the first new movie to star Kermit the Frog, Miss Piggy, and company in years, featured as its villain a guy named "Tex Richman." Tex was a sharp-dressed, smooth-talking oil executive who was, of course, vilified because he hated the environment. I decided to call out Hollywood for always going after evil businesspeople, and let's just say they didn't take the criticism too well.

On *Follow the Money,* my show on Fox Business at the time, I asked a simple question: Is liberal Hollywood using class warfare to brainwash our kids? I had a spirited discussion about that topic with my guests Dan Gainor of the Media Research Center and Andrea Tantaros, a cohost of mine on *The Five.* Dan pointed out that Hollywood had been indoctrinating our kids against corporations like this for years, and at one point quipped: "This is a Muppet movie for goodness' sakes! The only thing green on the screen should be Kermit!" Andrea agreed, saying, "I just wish liberals could leave little kids alone." It was a wide-ranging, lively discussion—we were even joined by liberal Professor Dr. Caroline Heldman of Occidental College, one of President Obama's alma maters, who offered her perspective. At one point, I offered a hypothetical: "Where are we," I asked. "Communist China?"

Well, that did it. The video of our discussion went viral, and liberals hit the roof. "The Muppets Are Communist, Fox Business Network Says," shrieked *The Huffington Post*. (I never actually said that, but who can expect them to get the story right?)[1] *Mother Jones* magazine felt the need to "get this straightened out" and assure their readers that *The Muppets* was not as bad as the Soviet propaganda movie *Battleship Potemkin*—a movie most *Mother Jones* readers are no doubt familiar with.[2] Across the pond, Tim Dowling, a columnist at *The Guardian,* said our discussion "threatened to usher in a whole new paradigm of stupid" but then spent the rest of his column mockingly looking for other Leftist influences in previous Muppet movies.[3] My old pal Jon Stewart joined in, calling it "the stupidest" controversy of that holiday season but nonetheless devoting five minutes of his own airtime to talking about it.

Even if the Muppets hadn't previously been used in environmentalist campaigns to "make Earth Day every day" (which they have); even if Kermit the Frog himself hadn't said it was "up to people" to "fix the damage they've caused to the earth" in a 1990 TV special (which he did);[4] you should still be able to talk freely about themes in a kids' movie that you find disturbing. However, liberal Hollywood wasn't having it. Any attempt to call out their long history of attacking business and profit and capitalism, and they circle the wagons and throw up their shields of outrage and snark. That's because, you see, I was attacking one of their core tenets.

In America today, the cornerstone belief among the Left is that "profit" has to be made a dirty word. Profit must be equated with selfishness, greed, and other manners of sin. And they've convinced a good chunk of the public of this belief by juxtaposing "the pursuit of profit" (and other related terms like "wealth," "capitalism," etc.) with nice-sounding words and phrases such as "income equality," "economic justice," and "fairness." "Inequality" has become the official buzzword of the Obama presidency and the central plank of the 2016 Democratic

Party platform. Sometimes you'll hear euphemisms like "level-ing the playing field" and "looking out for the middle class," but don't be deceived. What they are seeking is nothing less than the abolition of profit, the end of risk, the destruction of any incentive, and the creation of a society in which any value cre-ated by capitalists is confiscated and redistributed to those who didn't have a hand in it.

Take, for example, liberal icon Senator Elizabeth Warren, basically a female version of Bernie Sanders, who rails against "excessive" profits and urges higher taxes on corporations. "If America is going to build 21st Century infrastructure, operate 21st Century schools and invest in 21st Century research, then giant corporations must pay a fair share of the cost," she insists.[5]

That all sounds good, right? Until someone explains that these evil corporations are contributing to our economy right now: by creating millions of jobs for millions of people who pay taxes to support those twenty-first-century schools she's talking about. ExxonMobil alone employs 75,000 people. Walmart employs 1.4 million people[6] in this country, and while the work may not be glamorous or as well paid as some positions, it's honest, hon-orable work at wages set by the market—by the capitalist sys-tem itself. And each of those Walmart employees takes their wages and puts some of them back into the economy.

Pharmaceutical companies are funding billions in "21st Century research"—much of it on drugs that save people's lives—a feat Leftists like Elizabeth Warren believe should be penalized. Corporations aren't contributing their "fair share" to America? Well, what about the dirty kids who schlep around in tents protesting corporations instead of getting real jobs? Or interrupt campaign rallies with ignorant chants and demonstra-tions? What "fair share" are they contributing to their society?

For the record, here are some of the things corporate profits fund: hiring more employees, improving benefits to workers, expanding a business, returning money to shareholders (including elderly retirees with mutual funds), investing in life-improving technologies or life-saving research, saving money for a rainy day. None of these contributions are a consideration for the liberals wanting to tax corporate profits away. No, to liberals, every capitalist is a "robber baron" whose wealth is built at the expense of someone else, especially blue-collar workers and the poor.

In short, it is an ugly time to be a capitalist in the greatest capitalist nation on earth. Especially when you are attacked, defamed, and overregulated by a bunch of people who don't have any understanding of capitalism in the first place. Elizabeth Warren, for example, was a Harvard professor before she was a Senator. Barack Obama was a community organizer. They've never run a successful enterprise in the private sector in their lives. Take it from someone who cut his teeth in the private sector of America: The pursuit of profit is an ugly and beautiful thing. And it is the cornerstone of what makes this country the nation it is.

The harsh truth of my life is that without having that desire for profit, without possessing the ability to make more of myself than the lot I was born into, I'd have been condemned to a life of despair, anxiety, and misery. The pursuit of "profit" changed my life. Which is why I take the Left's effort to defame and distort the word very personally.

LEARNING THE BASICS

I learned about the power of profit early on. I had a lawn-care business as a kid, which kicked off a lifelong drive to always focus on improving my situation. I knew what I wanted, and I knew earning money felt great, but I still wasn't sure how it all *worked*. It was when I went to Rollins College that I got my first real lessons in how consumers behave and interact with the free market, and how to analyze that behavior to make money—in other words, capitalism. And the best of those lessons didn't come from economics class, they came from the chapter room at the Chi Psi Fraternity house.

My roommate during sophomore and junior year was a guy named Dave McCoy. We came from similar poor backgrounds—I grew up in Chicago, Dave in central Florida. Dave was the starting catcher on the Rollins baseball team while I started at third base. In addition to being nuts about baseball, we both knew that it was, in part, going to be our ticket out of being poor. It helped get us into college, and we knew we were lucky to be there—because more than anything, we both had a burning desire to rise above where we came from.

That meant Dave and I were always on the lookout for ways to make some extra cash. One day, Dave came into the fraternity house and told me he'd found a gas station that sold two-liter bottles of soda for 50 cents each. As long as you paid for a fill-up, you could get as many 50-cent two-liter sodas as you wanted! It was too easy. Soon Dave and I were making trip after trip to this gas station and buying loads of Coke, Sprite, orange soda, and anything else we could find, then turning around and selling it to our thirsty buddies on the baseball team or at the fraternity house for $1. We were doing great business, but after a while it got labor-intensive. It was tough to juggle our business—all those trips to the gas station, lugging the bottles, finding places to store our stock—along with class and baseball. We needed a shift in strategy, and if possible, an upgrade to increase our profit margin.

Then I had an idea. I remembered all the fun I'd had as a kid playing pinball—it was the kind of cheap entertainment I could afford growing up. I told Dave, why not take the profits from our soda hustle and buy a pinball machine? So we did. Yet this wasn't just for us to pass the time. We got an authentic coin-operated model, and set it up in the chapter room of the Chi Psi Fraternity house, where our buddies would come to hang out after—or sometimes during—class and on the weekends.

The guys didn't exactly take to the machine at first. It got some sporadic use, but we realized that if we were going to get a good return on our investment we would have to get more people spending their quarters on it. Brainstorming how to do that, I started to think about our target market, one we understood very well: young men in their late teens and early twenties, many of them college athletes. How to get guys like that interested in something? Answer: competition.

I wrote the top three high scores on a piece of paper, and posted it under the glass on the machine. The guys saw that, and the competitive instinct took over. Naturally, everyone wanted to beat the high score. Word spread, and soon there'd be five or six guys hanging around the machine all night trying to outdo each other! I had to keep updating the score sheet, and most importantly, the quarters were rolling in.

Our take got so big that Dave and I had to be careful about when we emptied the machine. If our buddies saw how much we were taking in, they might not be so free with their quarters. So we started emptying the machine in the middle of the night, when nobody was around. Every now and then Dave or I would empty it later on when there were more guys hanging around the chapter room, and when we knew there'd only be a few quarters in it. And for good measure, we'd say something like, "Oh, well, as long as everyone is enjoying the machine." Let's just say we weren't exactly publishing earnings reports. Even then, we knew not to underestimate the power of jealousy.

We killed it that year. And did Dave and I decide to blow it all like you might expect two crazy college kids to do? Nope. We never lost sight of our goal. Getting ahead—breaking out of poverty—was more important than partying. We decided to buy shares in Exxon—my first-ever venture into stocks. That set me off on the path to learning more about the market, and especially commodities, and here I am today! Yeah, I took a shot at being a big-league ballplayer, but after I got hurt, I remembered my early education in how understanding consumer behavior translates to understanding market behavior, which in turn translates to profit. And it was all thanks to my early business partner Dave McCoy and our friends in the Chi Psi Fraternity at Rollins.

SOMETIMES YOU'RE A SPIDER

In college, I thought I was going to end up playing baseball in the major leagues. That didn't happen, but years later I did find myself in the "big leagues" of capitalism, cutting my teeth in one of the toughest training grounds in the world economy: New York's commodities trading floor. This was capitalism in its purest, rawest form. I've seen it up close. And I'm not going to pretend it's always pretty, nice, or "fair." (There's a reason why Mark Zuckerberg is a billionaire who can espouse silly liberal ideas and the Winklevoss twins are just a couple of world-famous whiners, and it ain't necessarily because life is just.) Then again, as the great economist Milton Friedman once asked, what economic system is "fair?" Is communism fair? Or socialism? Aren't there always poor people and rich people anywhere you look?

The truth is that capitalism is one of the great equalizers in human society. Capitalism doesn't care, ultimately, who you are or where you come from. It's your ability to generate profit—which drives growth, jobs, and prosperity—that matters.

Most people don't appreciate what a blessing the free-market system—an American invention—was to the vast 99 percent of the world. Before America, in the days of monarchies, you had to have the permission of a ruler before you could own a business, or own land, or build an enterprise, or travel, or profit. Under the free enterprise system, you don't need anyone's permission to make a buck and provide for your family. Most people have forgotten about it now but in the 1970s, some American entrepreneurs made a fortune selling something called a "pet rock." It was just like it sounds. A foolish gift idea that became super trendy, like the Snuggie would decades later. But that's America for you. Even stupid ideas can work if you can sell them.

However, nothing quite oozes pure capitalism like the trading floors of New York. Here in this (sometimes) bloody capitalist jungle, I've seen grown men elbow each other—even get into in fistfights, as I did—on the commodities floor. I've seen traders in tears after losing their life's savings in a single day—something I experienced firsthand. And then weep tears of joy when they've made millions again a few weeks later. Let me tell you, there is nothing more purely American, more joyous, more heartless, more ruthless, or more egalitarian than the free market.

Trading commodities is one of the wildest rides you can have with your feet on the ground. As a trader, I saw friends go from multimillionaire "Masters of the Universe" who flew themselves to the Hamptons every weekend in their own planes to being dead broke and forced to work off their debts to a clearinghouse, all in one single day of bad trading.

I had my own ups and downs, too. This was the kind of place where taking a few hours off for important family time could cost you millions. Take, for example, when my son was in preschool. They liked to bring parents in every now and then to read to the class. When my turn came, one day in April, my wife and I had picked out a book called *The Spider and the Fly* to read to the children. Even if you don't know the whole story, you've probably heard the opening line:

"Will you walk into my parlor?" said the Spider to the Fly . . .

It may be a kids' book, based on a poem from the nineteenth century, but it is every bit as compelling today as it was when first written. The Spider smooth-talks the Fly, sensing her weaknesses, and draws her up the stairs into his parlor from which, as the story goes, "she never came out again."

The kids in my son's class listened with rapt attention, and once I was done, every little hand shot up with a question. So I found myself spending two hours deconstructing *The Spider and the Fly with twenty five-year-olds. How come the Spider tricked the Fly? Why did the Fly not know any better?* Their questions, and the answers I was forced to come up with on the spot, definitely made me think.

Eventually, story time came to an end, and I said good-bye to my son and headed over to the trading floor. What met me was a scene of pandemonium. It turned out an unexpected cold front had shot in from Canada that day, and the natural gas markets were going crazy as a result. My clerk met me with a look of horror: "Where have you been?" he asked. "Reading *The Spider and the Fly* with my son's class," I responded, calmly.

I'd lost $2 million already.

So I rolled up my sleeves and jumped into the pits. I made every dime of that $2 million back—that's how crazy the natural gas market was that day.

When you are a commodities trader, you never know what is going to cause a particular commodity to go haywire.

In the oil market, for instance, you've got to be prepared for anything, especially when there's conflict in the Middle East— and when is there not? That was the case on January 9, 1991. Saddam Hussein was threatening Kuwait, and President George H. W. Bush had sent then-Secretary of State James Baker over there to try and calm things down. The tension had oil trading at $23 a barrel, up from just $15 a barrel days before.

I was standing on the trading floor in the middle of the day when I saw three words flash a new headline on the *Dow Jones Newswires* ticker:

James Baker: "Regrettably . . ."

That was all we needed to see. Everyone standing around me holding orders for oil contracts had turned white. I looked into the other traders and saw nothing but fear. So, I decided to act.

"I'll buy your contracts," I said to the trader closest to me.

He looked at me like I was crazy. He was listing them at $28 a barrel, and asked me, "What do you mean you'll buy?" But I was serious—I took the contracts. "I don't know what you're going to do with them," he muttered, shaking his head as he signed the orders.

I had drawn him into my parlor like the unsuspecting Fly. I took all the contracts. And as the day went on, oil started skyrocketing—to $30, $33, $35, $38, and eventually $40 a barrel. By the end of the day, people were begging me to get those contracts back. It was one of the best trades I ever made. What can I say—sometimes you're the Spider, sometimes you're the Fly.

THE PURSUIT OF PROFIT: A BRIEF HISTORY

Both liberals and conservatives love to use Thomas Jefferson's famous phrase from the opening of the Declaration of Independence—"Life, Liberty and the pursuit of Happiness"—to back up their philosophical positions.

Liberals, however, forget one very important thing: Jefferson essentially cribbed that phrase from another Founding Father, George Mason, who in the Virginia Declaration of Rights cited "the enjoyment of life and liberty, with the means of acquiring and possessing property."[7] Mason, in turn, had borrowed it from philosopher John Locke's *Two Treatises of Government* ("preserve his property, that is, his life, liberty and estate").[8]

As you may have noticed, in both the previous usages, it is "property" that is a stand-in for Jefferson's "happiness." To Jefferson—indeed, to most if not all the Founders, who faced an illiberal, unrepresentative, high-tax, out-of-touch government (sound familiar?)—the pursuit of property and the pursuit of happiness were essentially the same thing. And how do you pursue property in a free society, without having profits? You can't.

This is the counterintuitive genius of free markets and the

profit motive: By being self-interested, we actually help create a better world. Yet liberals can't see past capitalism's raw grittiness and sharp elbows. They don't see the jobs created, the bills paid, the pride in earning wealth, getting a job, building something. I'll leave it to others to decide if this is willful ignorance or just plain stupidity (it's probably both).

As *The Economist* reported in June 2013, in the two decades between 1990 and 2010, the number of people living in "extreme poverty . . . fell by half as a share of the total population in developing countries, from 43% to 21%." These numbers represent nearly 1 billion people—a staggering number over such a short period of time. And "most of the credit," the magazine opined, must "go to capitalism and free trade, for they enable economies to grow—and it was growth, principally, that has eased destitution."[9]

The profit motive makes people work harder, take risks, and innovate new ideas that may create wealth for themselves—and jobs and economic growth for the folks in their community. Wanting to make money, take care of your family, and help grow the economy is nothing to be ashamed of. Amazingly, today we live in a country where the media, academia, and a significant portion of our elected leaders increasingly try to make us feel that it *is* shameful. And that, my friends, is the true shame. It is also one of the main reasons why the current debate over the minimum wage is such a hypocritical farce.

Across the country over the last couple of years, liberals have been calling for massive hikes in the minimum wage so that those working low-level jobs can have more "economic security." After all, there's too much profit for the fat cats. It's time people at the top make less, and people at the bottom make more. But here's the rub: Forcing companies to increase the pay of their lowest-skilled workers will indeed increase these workers' wages—right up until the day they are laid off because their employer can't afford to pay them anymore. How, exactly, does putting people out of work increase economic security?

Take the People's Republic of Seattle. In 2014, the city enacted a phased-in $15-an-hour minimum wage. The first phase of this monument to economic ignorance went into effect in April 2015 and will increase to $15 an hour by 2017. The effect?

According to an American Enterprise Institute (AEI) report from August 2015, which looked at just the restaurant sector, Seattle lost an estimated "1,000 restaurant jobs in May [2015] following the minimum wage increase in April [of that year]."

This represented that local industry's "largest one month job decline since a 1,300 drop in January 2009"[10] during the depths of the Great Recession. Meanwhile, between January and June, "restaurant employment nationally increased by 130,700 jobs" and "overall employment in the Seattle MSA [Metropolitan Statistical Area] increased 1.2% and by 21,800 jobs." And the real knockout data point? Restaurant employment in Washington state outside the Seattle MSA actually increased by 2,800 jobs (3.2 percent).[11]

These results should come as no surprise to anyone, even to liberal, chump economists like Paul Krugman, who make it sound like a minimum-wage increase is a panacea for poverty and their constant bugbear—wait for it—"inequality." If only those mean capitalist conservatives would stop being so stingy!

Let's be clear here—minimum wage jobs can be hard, thankless, and sometimes demeaning. I should know, I've held a few of my own. However, it's actually a good thing that these jobs suck—people should want and be encouraged to get out of these positions and pursue greater things. Flipping burgers and pouring coffee are occupational stepping-stones, not careers. There isn't much profit to be made in these jobs, but that's exactly the point.

When a man or woman or business generates wealth for themselves or itself, it can (and usually does) create wealth for others, too. Companies can't make products to sell without workers to make the products—so part of their wealth is passed along to workers in the form of wages. And these workers take these wages and buy necessities and luxuries from other sellers of goods, who turn around and take some of this generated wealth and pass it along to *their* employees. Of course, this is a simplification of a very complicated process, but it is apt: rising tides really do lift all boats, even the small ones.

THE "INCOME INEQUALITY" LIE

Today, the Left has become obsessed with so-called income in-equality. It's like a religion to them—though if it were an actual religion, they'd probably reject it. Yet can we ever have actual equality of income throughout an entire society? Of course not.

Decades ago, Lyndon B. Johnson declared an infamous "war on poverty" that was never won. Why? Because poverty never goes away. There will always be a group of people who are poor compared to a group of people who are rich. Inequality in regards to income is inevitable in all systems, even communism, which supposedly eliminated all economic classes. Remember those "party-member only" car lanes, limousines, dachas, and other luxuries enjoyed by the Communist Party elite in the Soviet Union? They represented just as much "income inequality" as a rich banker driving a Maserati down Rodeo Drive does today. The only difference is their rhetoric. And I'll take the honest American capitalist over a deceitful collectivist any day of the week. While there are some true believers on the Left who think total "fairness" and "equality" are achievable, the majority—at least in the media and political class—cynically use what they know is impossible to get people pissed off enough to vote for them or their favored candidates, even when it isn't in the economic interest of those people to do so.

Regardless of their intentions, liberals have created a dogmatic devotion to collectivist thinking, which centers on one primary "income" means to reach their "equality" ends: increasing taxes, especially on businesses and the wealthy. In fact, liberals often wax nostalgic about the "good ol' days" when the wealthiest of Americans paid about 90 percent in taxes. The standard liberal argument along these lines is something like, "Look at how high taxes were under Eisenhower, and the economy was booming!" These folks need both an economics and a history lesson.

First, while it is true that the U.S. economy generally did well in the 1950s (annual real GDP growth was 4.2 percent between 1950 and 1959), there were also four recessions between 1948 and 1961.[12] It wasn't all sunshine and roses in the U.S. economy during the Eisenhower Era.

Second, the U.S. economy's relative success in the 1950s had a lot to do with ours being the only major economy left standing after World War II, when we led the world in all kinds of economic indicators, often by historical margins. It was also a time when many of the major technological innovations of World War II were finally brought to market. We succeeded in the 1950s despite our tax code, not because of it.

Third, not many people actually paid the 90-plus-percent tax rate liberals like to cite as the reason for this American "golden age."[13] As Columbia University's Arpit Gupta wrote in a 2013 Manhattan Institute study, at that time, "very few people earned enough to meet the top rate threshold," and because of a variety of loopholes and tax incentives,[14] even "among those tax filers with the very highest incomes . . . the actual average tax rates were in fact comparable with today's."

But don't take my word for it—just listen to Thomas Piketty, the Left's prophet of inequality, in his 2007 paper, "How Progressive is the U.S. Federal Tax System? A Historical and International Perspective."[15]

The average individual income tax rate in 1960 reached an average rate of 31 percent at the very top, only slightly above the 25 percent average rate at the very top in 2004.

Within the 1960 version of the individual income tax, lower rates on realized capital gains, as well as deductions for interest payments and charitable contributions, reduced dramatically what otherwise looked like an extremely progressive tax schedule, with a top marginal tax rate on individual income of 91 percent.

In short, this high-tax "golden age" is as much a myth as a society's ability to achieve absolute equality.

Still, think about those who did face these unbelievable tax rates—up until the 1960s, nine out of every ten dollars they earned went to the government. What then was the motivation to succeed? There wasn't one. Such taxes sap the will of a people to reach for greatness, and for a nation to succeed economically, socially, and spiritually. Regardless of how many people actually paid them, it is a disgrace that taxes of this kind were ever on the books.

LIBERAL GREED:
Myths and Facts About the Left

I don't know about you, but I always love lectures about wealth and "economic justice" from multimillionaires who fly on private jets to exclusive conferences in Switzerland, or sip Chablis from the balcony of their mansions on the coasts. The truth is there is no creature more greedy, more profit hungry, and more purely capitalist than the limousine liberal who castigates the capitalist system from which they've squeezed every possible penny in order to earn votes or win applause from *The New York Times* (or both). I don't fault these characters for being greedy—I just like pointing out how their entire argument against the capitalist state is built on hypocrisy and lies.

Let's single out a few of the biggest offenders, whose reputations are built on myths concealing inconvenient facts.

MYTH: **Warren Buffett is a heroic billionaire working to make the capitalist system more just.**

Warren Buffett is every liberal's favorite billionaire. You rarely see the old codger anywhere unless it's sidling up to some Left-wing politician and telling the rest of America how much he can't wait for higher taxes on the wealthy.

FACT: **Warren Buffett is a total hypocrite.**

I love listening to famous liberals like Buffett rail on and on about capitalist greed and, once they've become extremely rich, suddenly demand higher taxes on everyone else. Now that he's made it, he's perfectly comfortable taxing the wealthy. And why not? He doesn't need any more money. I bet he wasn't demanding high taxes when he was just scraping together a living, though. In fact, I guarantee it.

And by the way, how did Warren Buffett first develop such a reputation for being a financial guru? It wasn't because he was out clothing the homeless. He put together a mammoth fund that helped a lot of people get extremely rich by betting on for-profit corporations. If Warren Buffett had his way, many of the corporations that made him filthy rich would be taxed out of existence.

MYTH: **Liberal Mark Zuckerberg is giving his vast wealth to charity.**

In the winter of 2015, Facebook founder and cutthroat capitalist Zuckerberg (a guy who reportedly sabotaged his own friends to take full control of his company) announced he was giving 99 percent of his vast wealth to charity. This was widely applauded by the Left and liberal outlets, like *The New York Times,* as a demonstration of how all money-grubbing capitalists should behave.[16] *The Times* called it a sign of "the latest indication of a growing interest in philanthropy among Silicon Valley's young billionaires."[17] Let the masses benefit from "excess" wealth.

FACT: **Zuckerberg is a calculating capitalist wanting to hold on to his profits.**

Within days, the liberal world learned the bitter truth. Zuckerberg wasn't actually giving his money to a charity, but a new company that would allow him to still use his vast wealth any way he wanted—like donating to Left-wing political campaigns. Zuckerberg's true plan, as one critic put it, was "to keep all of my wealth and use a lot of it to make the world a better place, as long as I get to define 'a lot' and 'better.' "[18] As CBS News reported, "Facebook has used a range of accounting techniques to minimize its taxes. Those include funneling profits to tax havens overseas, a practice critics say deprives the U.S. government of revenue."[19] Turns out the great philanthropist is a true capitalist after all.

MYTH: **Fat, slovenly reprobate scumbag Michael Moore is an anticapitalist.**

Anyone remember this clown? Moore is this total loser who got attention for a few years by making films extolling socialists like the murdering psychopaths running Cuba; or attacking corporations like General Motors that made the mistake of giving him a job before he quit after one day because, well, work is hard, and he likes to pretend he's some sort of Left-wing anticapitalist lunatic.

FACT: **Michael Moore is a fervent capitalist (though it is true he is also a fat, slovenly reprobate scumbag).**

The cruel and beautiful irony of the capitalist system is that it allowed Michael Moore to become a multimillionaire with films railing against the very system that made his personal wealth possible. He lives not in some ghetto where he gives all of his earnings to his fellow proletariats, but in a Manhattan high-rise far above the great unwashed.[20] Only in a free society is such hypocrisy allowed. If it weren't, we'd have to lock up most of Hollywood, three-quarters of Washington, D.C., pretty much all the mainstream media, and a good chunk of the elites in Manhattan, Chicago, Los Angeles, Boston, and San Francisco.

MYTH: "Feminist" heroes like Meryl Streep care deeply about "income inequality."

A 2015 headline read, "Meryl Streep Decries Income Inequality in Hollywood."[21] And at the 2015 Academy Awards, Streep rose to her feet and obnoxiously whistled in support of actress Patricia Arquette who said it was time to have wage equality "once and for all!" Streep told reporters it was "our responsibility" to make this happen.[22]

FACT: Meryl Streep likes income inequality just fine, thank you.

By "income inequality," was Ms. Streep referring to the vast disparity between what is paid to actors versus members of the film crew? No, she meant between how much male actors are paid versus female actors. Let's take a look at Matt Damon and Meryl Streep, for example. Matty's worth a cool $90 million,[23] while critics' sweetheart Meryl is worth "only" $75 million.[24] These celebrities—like many of their peers—make millions or tens of millions of dollars per movie. At the same time, the average salaries of the electrical, lighting, camera, and sound professionals that help them make these movies all average well under $100,000 per year.[25] This sure doesn't seem "equal" or "fair" to me. And I'm sure it doesn't to these film crew folks, either.

But Ms. Streep's heroic stand is a perfect example of the essentially warped nature of modern liberalism: She's fighting the good fight! So that one set of millionaires can be treated as equally as another set of millionaires! Can't you just smell the Nobel Prize, Meryl? You're a real Mother Teresa.

By the way, how much of her own salary does Ms. Streep forgo to return to the little people of the film industry? Unless we've all missed something, she's given them a total of *zero* dollars and a pile of nonsense.

MYTH: **Bernie Sanders is a socialist.**

It also allows Comrade Bernie Sanders, our socialist Senator from Vermont, to build a mini-empire on the Left by railing against a system in which he's done quite well. Here's what Comrade Sanders had to say on wealth and "income inequality" in a May 2015 interview with MSNBC's John Harwood (one of the most blatantly biased liberal media hacks out there):

> Ninety-nine percent of all new income generated today goes to the top 1 percent. The top one-tenth of 1 percent owns as much wealth as the bottom 90 percent. Does anybody think that that is the kind of economy this country should have? Do we think it's moral? So to my mind, if you have seen a massive transfer of wealth from the middle class to the top one-tenth of 1 percent, you know what, we've got to transfer that back if we're going to have a vibrant middle class. And you do that in a lot of ways. Certainly one way is tax policy.[26]

FACT: **Bernie Sanders just plays a socialist on TV.**

Bernie Sanders has a net worth that's pushing a million dollars ($700,000)[27] and makes an annual salary of $174,000 a year[28]—about 3.5 times as much as the U.S. median annual income.[29] This is our "Tribune of the People"? Will Sanders himself choose to "feel the Bern" of giving away what is by average standards a *lot* of money, both in terms of net worth and annual income? The hypocrisy of the Left would be utterly astounding if it weren't so consistently thrown in our faces.

Do the tens of millions of dollars he raised for his 2016 presidential campaign from his citizen-socialists—promptly handed over to huge corporations to run TV ads—keep him up at night? Unlikely. Where's the "economic equality" in that? It's like "economic inequality" everywhere: It's a fantasy.

MYTH: **Hillary Clinton is fighting for economic "fairness."**
Hillary Clinton has said on the campaign trail, "I believe we have to build a growth-and-fairness economy. You can't have one without the other."

FACT: **Hillary Clinton's definition of fairness is what's fair for her.**
Is it "fair" that Hillary Clinton can write a book that hardly anyone reads and still earn millions of dollars before a single copy was sold? A lot of people would consider this grossly unfair—why does she deserve compensation that is unhinged from the actual sales of her book (and the free market)? But don't hold your breath waiting for Mrs. Clinton to give all that money back in the name of economic "justice."

Is it fair that she and her husband collect tens of millions in speaking fees as a reward for their public service? Did Americans vote for the Clintons in the 1990s so that they could be among the richest people in America today? And in all of her lectures about greed on Wall Street, is it "fair" that Wall Street banks are some of her biggest campaign contributors?[30] Wonder what's in it for them.

GREED IS GOOD

I don't fault our liberal betters for taking advantage of the capitalist system. I just fault them for lying to themselves and to others about exactly what they are doing in order to service their nutty political agenda.

Now that they've profited from the capitalist system, and have every intention to keep what is theirs, the elites of the Left still feel free to lecture the rest of the world about the evils of profit seeking. But make no mistake: These are very greedy people—more greedy in fact than conservatives. Though conservative households statistically have 6 percent less income than liberal households, conservatives give on average 30 percent more than liberals to charity.[31]

Ironically the only way to keep America the country that has allowed the Barbra Streisands and Chers and Matt Damons and Jon Stewarts of the world to become rich and successful is to ignore their BS rants altogether. And to remember what made our nation the most prosperous nation on earth. Put another way, Americans are a naturally capitalistic people. It's in our blood—our DNA. Even those who claim to think capitalism is evil are willing participants—as long as they are the sole beneficiaries.

I'm a capitalist and proclaim that loudly and proudly.

3. MANLINESS

noun man·li·ness   \\'man-lē-nəs\\

(1.) the set of qualities considered appropriate for or character-istic of men

—Merriam-Webster's definition

(1.) the last impediment to a gender-neutral society, and the final refuge of white, cisgendered patriarchy

(2.) an anachronistic set of behaviors that are the hallmark of male privilege

—A Leftist's definition

The old iron days have gone, the days when the weakling died as the penalty of inability to hold his own in the rough warfare against his surroundings. We live in softer times. . . . We need then the iron qualities that must go with true manhood. We need the positive virtues of resolution, of courage, of indomitable will, of power to do without shrinking the rough work that must always be done.

—THEODORE ROOSEVELT, COLORADO SPRINGS,

AUGUST 2, 1901

Men, have you ever held a door open for a woman? Women, have you ever let a man loan you his coat because you were cold? Do you believe that women should be rescued from a collapsing building before men?

If so, congratulations—you are a blatant sexist! At least, that's according to one new, supposedly groundbreaking study. And for some reason it matters that a star of the Harry Potter films feels the same way.

You might know the actress Emma Watson as Hermione

Granger, the precocious female lead in the movies of the J. K. Rowling novels. She is also something called the UN Women Goodwill Ambassador. Yes, at the age of twenty-five, the United Nations has declared her an expert on how men and women should treat one another. And she's very serious about it—when she isn't promoting her movies or her cover shoots in *Vogue*.

"Chivalry should be consensual,"[1] Watson declared. A man can open a door for her, she says, but only if he would allow her to open the door for him. She described a recent date where she insisted on paying for dinner (something that she, as a millionaire, didn't have a problem doing), leading to an "awkward" discussion of gender roles.[2]

Along those same lines, a "first of its kind" study conducted in Boston in 2015 declared that any act of male chivalry is "benevolent sexism." Men who exhibit displays of gallantry— sadly, an increasingly outdated word—"are hindering gender equality." A nice guy, as one article put it, "is just a wolf in sheep's clothing."[3] In other words, every man is the enemy.

Let's all hope a man and woman aren't trapped in a burning building together anytime soon. Under our new gender rules, they'd both burn to death while they debated who would get to exit the room first. "After you." "No, after you." "No, really, I insist."

The gender-neutral society. Women equal to men. A society where one's place, duties, or rights aren't judged by what's under their clothing, but by the content of their character. Doesn't sound so bad, does it? It's a pretty uncontroversial thing these days.

No one seems to object to a gender-blind society. Getting to that promised land has nowhere near the opposition that, say, desegregation efforts faced in the days when a brave woman named Rosa Parks sat in the front of a bus or a preacher named Martin Luther King Jr. sat in a Birmingham jail. There have been no presidential contenders running on a single-issue platform opposing "equal rights" for women.

Unfortunately, radical feminists' pursuit of a gender-neutral society has gone too far. It's come with a cost. They've tried erasing differences in human nature that simply can't be erased. They've instead foisted on us a vision of the so-called modern male that lacks any masculinity. In sum, they've tried—and if our popular culture is any judge, succeeded—in stamping out manliness. (The very word has become provocative, even toxic in some quarters, which is why it's the title of this chapter.)

Now, before I start getting called a knuckle-dragging women-hater, a Bull Connor of the twenty-first century unleashing fire hydrants to extinguish the dreams of young women who want to become astronauts, doctors, and lawyers, let me clarify something: Women ought to pursue their dreams. And no man ought to be what stands in her way. Unfortunately, however, we're creating a society where those dreams, as defined by Hollywood and the gaggle of pantsuited radicals, can't include motherhood, nursing, or teaching. Or any of the other occupations or activities (and yes, that includes raising kids) that women have undertaken for centuries. My mother worked hard every day— she had one job during the week and another on weekends. She did this because she had to, so our family could survive financially. She didn't do it because she was embarrassed about being a mom, or because she was told that staying home with her family was not a job, but a "hobby."[4]

Tell me the last time you heard the phrase "as American as motherhood and apple pie." It's probably been a while. When the latter isn't being confiscated by the anti-trans-fat brigades led by Michael Bloomberg, the former is under constant assault by radical feminists who see mothers as helpless victims of patriarchy and children as chains to keep women at home. It's no wonder they support Planned Parenthood: 327,000 abortions performed in one year[5] means 327,000 fewer opportunities for women to be tied down with domestic responsibilities for a child.

The jihad for gender neutrality has claimed many victims, but none has as far-reaching an impact on American society as the eradication of manliness and the feminist effort to make our men more sensitive, empathetic, and nurturing—in short, more like women. Eliminating "manliness" is the final obstacle to creating the gender-neutral society.

IN PRAISE OF MASCULINITY

Manliness isn't unchecked bravado. It's not about getting into bar fights. Or belching in public. Or generally acting like an ass. It certainly does, however, allow for a little bragging, a little proud cockiness in the right circumstances. In the right situation. Like on the gridiron or baseball diamond.

I was the starting third baseman for Rollins College when our coach, who used to scout for the Pittsburgh Pirates, talked their major league team into coming to Winter Park to dedicate a new baseball stadium we had just built. Baseball greats like Tony Peña, Bobby Bonilla, Dale Berra were all there. They were having a good laugh at us college kids trying to play their game.

I led off the top of the second inning with a blast way over the left field wall. Don Robinson, their number one pitcher, was on the mound, and I'd just nailed one off him. Suddenly, the big leaguers weren't laughing anymore. On my next at bat, I crushed another Robinson pitch, this time to deep center field, and Bonilla had to reach over the fence to make the catch.

I knew I was going to be drafted after that day.

I could've been intimidated by these guys. Probably I should have been. Yet I had the guts, the cojones, to do my own thing as best I could, despite all that. That's what men do. That's what manliness is all about.

Ask any normal person whose mind has not been polluted by the poison peddled by the Leftist feminists and they will tell you that to be a man, one must be brave. Manliness is the sober knowledge that in fact there is no such thing as a "safe space" in this world. The best we can do is to prepare for all reasonable eventualities and teach the same to our children.

When I was a boy, I can remember all of us piling into our car. We were headed out on a road trip. Inevitably a few hours in, my mom would be frantic. Between my parents in the front seat would be a map, which my father would try to steal glances at as he gripped the wheel. My mom would plead with him to pull over and ask for directions. My dad would refuse. His independence, pride, and stubbornness wouldn't allow it. Most of us who are old enough to remember a time before Google Maps and Waze can remember moments like this.

Dad was a manly man. He didn't like asking for help. He felt in control—and wanted to convey control—when it looked like he was lost or out of his element. It was confidence, some might say bravado, that he was independent and it gave confidence to the rest of us, with the possible exception of my mother, who had seen the routine a few too many times.

But my dad understood that a man must possess a mature set of priorities. This does not include endless hours playing video games while someone spoon-feeds you sugared cereal. A quiet strength helps. A man can take care of himself. But that is only half of what it means to be a man. Being a man also means you are willing to spend your courage sticking up for others who are vulnerable or less fortunate than you. Being a man means not only that you can take care of yourself, but also that you try to take care of others as well. Being a man means that you suppress your own feelings and urges out of respect for other people's wishes or whatever is best for them. Never punishing your kid out of anger, for example, is a sign of manliness. That ties in with the general drive to put your family before anything else in the world—the greatest thing a man can do.

Sometimes being a man means knowing when you're beat. I've learned that lesson plenty of times on the baseball field. Yet after every game I lost, I always tried to learn something. It was the same every time I had a bad day on the trading floor, and lost huge amounts of money. That lesson was reinforced to me in an unorthodox way by a good friend and mentor from my commodities trading days, Mark Fisher.

For the eighteen years I was on the trading floor, Mark taught me a ton, not just about commodities but about life. I could fill a whole book with his teachings. I was eager to learn from him because he was a model of success, and simply a good man—he had a boatload of money and a heart the same size. He also had a great sense of humor. One day, out of the blue, in front of a bunch of hotshot traders, Mark challenged me to a footrace. The stakes? Ten thousand dollars to a charity of the winner's choosing. Here I was, a former pro athlete, still in good shape (to this day I run fifteen to twenty miles a week and work out)—and there was Mark, older than I was and a bit pudgy. At first I thought he was joking. When I realized he was serious, I asked him if he wanted a head start. Nope, he said, but he wanted to pick the time and place for the race. We had a deal.

I forgot about Mark's wager for a while. We had a lot going on. Then, we came to the end of a particularly crazy trading day. The gas market had been jumping all over the place, thanks to a hurricane brewing in the Caribbean that threatened U.S. gas production. By the time the closing bell rang, I was drenched in sweat and physically exhausted. Then I looked up—and there was Mark. Wearing a pair of cleats. He announced to the entire trading pit that the race for $10,000 was on—right now.

So, we headed outside, Mark and I and a whole crowd of traders and clerks who just couldn't wait to see what happened. I was tired, but I was still in much better shape than Mark. I figured I had this in the bag—after all, we'd agreed on only a thirty-five-yard length for the race. We headed out to the "course," which was a grassy area along the side of One World Trade Center. When we stepped onto the grass, I realized something was up. The grass was way higher than usual. It was up to about six inches. I was wearing work shoes . . . and Mark was in his cleats. I found out later that he had paid the landscapers to *not* cut that grass for three weeks. Nice trick, I thought, but I still shrugged it off. No way he could beat me.

We took our positions at the starting line, and Mark took off a split second before the word "Go." Even then, I thought, a little head start won't help him much. I'm the former pro athlete here! But as it turned out, running in work shoes in that long grass took away any physical advantage I had. The brief head start hadn't helped. Halfway through the race I looked over and Mark—in his cleats—was ahead of me. He beat me—just barely— and all of our fellow traders got a real kick out of it. The short, pudgy, older guy had beaten the hotshot former ballplayer.

I accepted the call despite Mark's shenanigans—after all, we were and still are good friends. Some might say that the "manly" thing to do would have been to make a big stink about it—to protest the race and refuse to pay up. However, I couldn't help admiring Mark's brilliance. He had set up the situation to make up for—and surpass—the natural physical advantages that I held over him. And he'd won.

Mark doesn't know it, but because of that lesson, I consider myself the real winner. I learned that with clever strategic planning, you can eliminate your competitor's advantage. Of course, that lesson was right there in the Bible the whole time—David can defeat Goliath with the right tools. I just had to learn it for myself, and that lesson has paid for itself many times over.

Men are natural competitors, and part of being a good man is knowing how to lose and learning from your losses. Mark Fisher and I had a good laugh, remained friends—today he's godfather to my son—and soon went back to the business of working hard to provide for our families. Because that, at the end of the day, is what men do.

I know, I know. This all sounds very sexist and un-PC. The only thing more reviled than "manning up" in this world, is the dreaded charge of "paternalism." That is the true kiss of death in modern society. But you know what I say? Too bad.

After all, we get to hear endlessly about Hillary Clinton running as the champion of feminism. Like the whole point of her political campaign is to throw off the yoke of evil paternalism.

But here's what I don't get: Hillary Clinton wouldn't even be here if not for her husband. She is who she is because she married the right man. And by "right man," I do *not* mean she married an actual "good man," at least not in the traditional sense of manliness. Not only is Hillary Clinton a terrible face for "feminism," she is the most infamous apologist for philandering husbands in American history. Her husband has been accused of raping women. Countless accusations of sexual harassment, in the workplace and elsewhere, have been made against him. And, perhaps the most despicable of all, her husband took scurrilous advantage of his position—the highest office in the land—to prey upon a vulnerable intern just a few years older than his own teenaged daughter and "have relations" with her in the Oval Office. And then broke the poor girl's heart and left her to twist in the wind of his lies and denials, as the jackals in the press tore her to shreds. There is nothing manly about that and there is nothing feminist about covering for it. Both Clintons should have been drummed out of public office long ago.

Manliness is best described by those who exude it. Think about the courage of the members of SEAL Team Six, who run toward danger, rather than from it. Think of the accountability demanded by a CEO like Jack Welch. Think of the brooding confidence of *Casablanca*'s Humphrey Bogart with a cigarette at the bar. Think of the reassuring steel and quiet command of Margaret Thatcher, who told President George H. W. Bush, "This is no time to go wobbly, George," when Saddam Hussein invaded Kuwait in 1990. Yes, a woman can exude "manliness," too.

The truth is—and you won't learn this on a college campus in America today—every shining moment in American history has been defined by manliness. When Jamestown was settled in

1607, it was manliness that gave the settlers the strength, courage, and determination to grab hold of their wild new frontier
thousands of watery miles from home and never let it go. It was
the pure manliness of General George Washington that allowed
him to lead his ragtag troops through frigid winters to win the
unlikeliest of victories against the greatest standing army on
earth at the time. It was George Washington's manliness that
led him to surrender his battle sword and leave his military command to become America's first President.

The fact is, there is an inherent manliness to the American
experience. It's a virtue that built our nation. Rugged pioneers
who defended their land with guns—from colonials, from intruders, from land grabbers, from charlatans. Abigail Adams
spoke out on political issues when it wasn't deemed a woman's
place. Dolley Madison saved some of the nation's treasures after
the White House was set on fire.

It was a manly devotion to the mission at hand that guided
Abraham Lincoln to preserve the union and finally end the
scourge of slavery. And it was unrivaled manliness in so many
of our Greatest Generation who left farms, small towns, and a
few big cities in America for far-off foreign lands to jump out
of airplanes and storm beaches, to die and be grievously wounded
in the great effort of lopping the head off the insatiable Nazi
regime and Japanese imperialism.

In later years, Rosa Parks had the guts to do what many others
feared—to expose the idiocy of racism in the 1960s. Boy, I
would put Rosa Parks or any one of those pioneer women up
against the toughest-talking frat boy in any American college
today. Even with a hand tied behind her back, I would bet on
any one of those women.

Manliness, as Harvard sociologist and political philosopher
Harvey Mansfield defines it, is "confidence in the face of risk."[6]
Manliness consists of courage, assertiveness, directness, loudness,
protectiveness, stoicism, aggressiveness, dominance, and a host
of other characteristics that are traditionally thought to belong

to men. Again, this is not to say that women can't display these qualities. They do, and some women do quite often, but over the entire population, they tend to be present in men more often than women.

But manliness isn't just about what's in our DNA. It's about how we raise our kids, and how we teach them to become adults. And that's what we're losing these days. Consider Theodore Roosevelt, undoubtedly the most manly President to ever occupy the Oval Office. He was living proof of the idea that manliness was a virtue that could be taught and cultivated. He was born with asthma and constantly bedridden. His father told him that unless he was constantly exercising, exploring the great outdoors, and pushing his physical boundaries and strength, he would remain sickly. Teddy started boxing regularly. He shot bears and dangerous game. In a near-suicidal episode, he led men into battle up San Juan Hill.

Can you imagine how Teddy Roosevelt would react to *The New York Times* when in 2015 it helpfully offered twenty-seven ways to be a "modern man," including how to use a melon baller, and how to buy shoes for his spouse: "When the modern man buys shoes for his spouse, he doesn't have to ask her sister for the size. And he knows which brands run big or small."[7] *Spoiler alert*: The best way to be a modern man? Be a woman.

These days we are seeing the "wussification" of the American male, and God help any man who stands up to it. As the ever-classy Senator Claire McCaskill put it, men should "shut the hell up"[8]—a playful slam on men that the mainstream media loved. Men are turned into metrosexuals, with perfect manicures, hair just so, and colorful socks. Justin Bieber dresses and talks and wears his hair like a girl.

Supporters of President Obama's health-care law outdid themselves around Christmastime 2013, in their campaign to get young Millennials going home for the holidays to talk up all the great (promised) benefits of government health with their crotchety and (wisely) suspicious parents and relatives. The President's never-ending campaign arm tweeted out a picture of a young man, clearly lounging around the house in his pajamas for the holidays. His hands are cupping a mug. The caption in a green space beside the picture read: "Wear pajamas. Drink hot chocolate. Talk about getting health insurance."[9] It looked like a Christmas card.

It also looked like, well, the end of man. Clearly, the man-boy was fully mature, physically. Thick black curls and shaved chin with man-sized, if soft and unblemished, hands cradle the hot chocolate. Christmas lights twinkle in the background. He is sitting on a plush leather sofa—the kind only your parents could afford. And he is wearing pajamas. Not just any pajamas, but onesie, zip-up pajamas—like the little outfits infants wear. Only instead of yellow giraffes or pink hippos, the man-child who became known as "pajama boy" is wearing zippered pajamas patterned after a lumberjack's black and red flannel shirt. You know, the kind that strong men with giant axes wear when chopping, splitting, and hauling firewood to heat their home for their family. The image of such a burly and bearded man could not be any more discordant when compared with the smug, self-satisfied, eyebrow-arched face gazing over the top of his hot chocolate. Pajama boy is saying: "Yes. I am physically post-puberty. I have never lifted an axe or roughed my hands against the splinters of firewood. I have never heated a home. But you will pay for my health care." Welcome, America, to the Modern Man.

Trigger warning: The phrases that follow may cause heartburn, hives, hot flashes, or fainting spells. "Man up!" "Act like a man!" Is there anything deemed more hateful on college campuses in America today than telling someone to "man up"? In the fall, University of San Diego held a seminar titled "Man Up? Masculinity and Pop Culture." It was sponsored by the campus's "Women's Center." It was described thusly: "This workshop invites men to engage in a cultural analysis of how masculinity is represented, and how that representation frequently has negative repercussions on men's lives."[10] College-aged men in America were once taught how to tune up a car, skin a deer, and how to pin a flower on the strap of a date's dress without sticking her. Today, they are taught to "engage in a cultural analysis of how masculinity is represented." Good grief.

Even far away from Left Coast crazy colleges, "manning up" or "acting like a man" is treated like a hate crime. The University of Nebraska—located in a state that's home to some of the toughest men in America, thanks to husking all that corn and surviving those brutal winters—has succumbed to the same nonsense. Last year, the university declared the phrase "man up" to be tantamount to calling a gay person "homo" or a mentally handicapped person "retarded." As part of a campaign to thwart all the hatefulness, volunteers wore bright pink shirts warning students that saying "man up" only "reinforces masculine stereotypes that are unhealthy for everyone."[11] Unhealthy? Everyone? Lord, help us! Even the elite Duke University in North Carolina banned the phrase "man up" after lumping it in with words like "fag."[12]

What is really perverse is how these universities take our young people at one of the most impressionable phases of their lives and then poison them with this nonsense. And then send parents the bill! Or, even worse, saddle students with a lifetime of debt—all for the privilege of getting your mind and soul totally ruined! When you first think about all of this claptrap that colleges instill in our young people, it sounds just silly. Goofy. Something funny that all the rest of us can have a big laugh over.

However, there is nothing funny about it. It is very, very serious. These universities are not just setting these students up to be ridiculous failures in life, too terrified to take risks, too weak to survive failure, and completely unable to deal with adversity. They are not just teaching young men to grow up to be sissified wimps who wear tight suits and skinny jeans. (I tried to put on a pair of skinny jeans once—it would've taken two of those pant legs just to fit one of mine!) The worst part of it is that the universities are twisting the very definition of what it means to be a man and literally perverting manhood into something that is evil and corrupt. They've turned it into something that is quite honestly the opposite of what manhood is supposed to be and what it always has been.

In Ohio, a six-year-old boy was suspended from school for pretending to shoot his friend with a bow and arrow.[13] You know, like kids have done for decades before the PC police showed up to terrorize playgrounds across America. There's a war on football—see Will Smith's movie *Concussion*—part of a continual effort to demonize competitive sports in America. "Football has become soft," Donald Trump proclaimed to a cheering crowd, discussing the rise of penalty flags to discourage any "rough" tackling. "Just like America has become soft."[14]

And then there's Stefonknee Wolschtt. The Canadian transgender was forty-six years old and had been married to a woman for twenty-three years, with whom he had seven children, when he decided he was no longer a man. He was, in fact, a six-year-old little girl. Alarmed, his wife told him to straighten up or hit the road. He grabbed his crazy bags and left so that he could freely dress up as a six-foot-two-inch, porky six-year-old girl, with pink bows in her ringlets of hair. And, sure enough, she was able to find a couple to adopt her so she could live honestly as a six-year-old little girl. No word on whether this new life involves recognizing birthdays or if Stefonknee Wolschtt will remain six years old forever.

You pick up *The New York Times* and read about Caitlyn Jenner's "courage" for going from living as a rich and famous man to living as a rich and famous woman. "Good for Jenner. All this is probably harder than the training for the Olympic decathlon—but more important, because transgender people face hate crimes and discrimination at an astonishing rate," wrote the allegedly serious journalist Nicholas Kristof in the august pages of *The New York Times*.[15] Yes, this is the same newspaper that in the same pages denounced the truly great tragic hero Chris Kyle of *American Sniper* fame as "insane."[16]

Caitlyn Jenner is considered a "hero"—for what, exactly? Coming out as transgender—with the full support of Hollywood, the mainstream media, and enormous reservoirs of fame and wealth? A more likely hero is a fifteen-year-old boy who's thrown out of his house because he stood up to his dad while his dad's beating up his mother—because any person of the male gender who hits a woman does not deserve to be called a man, and is in fact something subhuman altogether. What about the gay kid who comes out even though he knows some bullies at school are going to try to beat the crap out of him? That kid has guts. Not some pampered millionaire(ss?) who's already the toast of the town, and gets a *Vanity Fair* spread for deciding to be a seventy-year-old woman. It's crazy.

Only a culture this backward could somehow anoint Hillary Clinton as a feminist icon. This woman makes it her business to ignore or denigrate the women who have accused her husband of sexual assaults, yet she still has the gall to declare that "every survivor of sexual assault deserves to be heard, believed, and supported." Unless of course, they are women like Juanita Broaddrick and Paula Jones who threaten the Clinton empire and who should, in that case, not only *not* be "heard, believed, and supported" but dismissed, ridiculed, and savaged by the Clinton propaganda machine. In her latest strategy, she's decided to adopt "blame-men-first feminism," which earned her the criticism of actual feminist Camille Paglia.[17] I guess men are just easy targets these days.

But it's not just pop culture or politics that we have to blame. This kind of thing starts right in our own homes. Parents, influenced by politicians and celebrities who tell them that "boys being boys" are doing something wrong, silently accept these radical changes. They don't have the guts to sit their kids down for frank, honest talk about the way things are versus the way they should be. The way they *used* to be. If enough American parents had these talks with their kids, we'd have a shot at reclaiming our country's greatness.

IN DEFENSE OF FEMININITY

"Being powerful is like being a lady," Britain's Prime Minister Margaret Thatcher once said. "If you have to tell people you are, you aren't." Thatcher—who was such a feared anticommunist that the Soviets called her the Iron Lady (not the Iron Person or the Iron Human)—never hid her femininity. She used it, to charm dictators, and Cabinet members, and her American counterpart, Ronald Reagan. She wore dresses and hats and carried a purse. So did another influential British female—Queen Elizabeth II. They follow a long tradition of strong, independent, but decidedly feminine women, from Cleopatra to Joan of Arc to Queen Victoria.

These days, however, being feminine is as bad as being masculine. In fact, being feminine is even worse. Increasingly, women are trained to emulate the most shocking behavior and furthest bounds of sexual freedom. In the 1990s, this was exemplified by feminist icon Roseanne Barr grabbing her crotch while singing the National Anthem at a baseball game. More recently, it's been women shedding dresses, purses, or anything indicating femininity—the rise of the so-called power suit.

In 2013, a study of two thousand working women found that 25 percent dressed masculinely because in their view it was the only way to be treated seriously. Another quarter wore less makeup to work for similar reasons. Forty-two percent said that senior women at their companies acted like "alpha females" to get ahead—assuming traditionally male characteristics.[18] Under the Obama administration, we now have women in combat roles for the first time in our history.

THE FACTS OF BIOLOGY

We are afraid to admit the basic facts of biology: men and women are different. Walk into a hospital and you'll find most of the nurses are women, 93 percent by one count.[19] Car mechanics are 98 percent men.[20] How to explain this? Is it some patriarchy keeping women down by ensuring they get nowhere near a monkey wrench? Of course not.

The social engineers of the Left ignore the basic facts of biology. If you're born with two X chromosomes (a female), instead of an X and Y chromosome (a male), what you may lack in size and strength, you tend to make up for in dexterity and endurance—women generally live longer. Given these facts of biology, men have an evolutionary instinct to protect those they think are more vulnerable. There are still vestiges of this in some customs like opening doors for women, walking closest to the curb, or giving up a jacket or sweater on a chilly night. This used to be called "gallantry"—a word almost as endangered as "mankind."

Radical feminists and a complacent media are so afraid to admit this, in fact, that our society has gone out of its way to satisfy every possible definition of gender. In 2014, Facebook listed fifty-six gender options for its users. Here's the list:

- Agender
- Androgyne
- Androgynous
- Bigender
- Cis
- Cisgender
- Cis Female
- Cis Male
- Cis Man
- Cis Woman
- Cisgender Female
- Cisgender Male

- Cisgender Man
- Cisgender Woman
- Female to Male (FTM)
- Gender Fluid
- Gender Nonconforming
- Gender Questioning
- Gender Variant
- Genderqueer
- Intersex
- Male to Female (MTF)
- Neither
- Neutrois
- Non-binary
- Other
- Pangender
- Trans
- Trans★[21]
- Trans Female
- Trans★ Female
- Trans Male
- Trans★ Male
- Trans Man
- Trans★ Man
- Trans Person
- Trans★ Person
- Trans Woman
- Trans★ Woman
- Transfeminine
- Transgender
- Transgender Female
- Transgender Male
- Transgender Man
- Transgender Person
- Transgender Woman
- Transmasculine

- Transsexual
- Transsexual Female
- Transsexual Male
- Transsexual Man
- Transsexual Person
- Transsexual Woman
- Two-Spirit

A college in California now allows students to choose from six genders.[22] Not to be outdone, the State University of New York offers seven.[23] Harvard University will now allow students to choose their own gender-neutral identifiers—so professors can refer to students as "he" or "she" or "ze "or "hir" or "hirs."[24]

Forget for a moment just the basic issue of how many bathrooms need to be built to manage this new gender math. It's no wonder we lack any respect for manliness. We can't even figure out what gender we belong to anymore. It's whatever a man or a woman or a "two-spirit" or a "ze" decides they feel like that day.

Of course, even Harvard knows this is all an unworkable mess. As a *Boston Globe* article on their much-lauded policy change later noted, "the change will not affect the students' overall gender assignment, meaning each student will still be classified as a male or female by the college, regardless of preferred pronoun."[25]

For all the efforts to enforce these unusual norms, radical feminists haven't succeeded—yet.

4. THRIFT

noun \'thrift\

(1.) careful use of money so that it is not wasted
—Merriam-Webster's definition

(1.) an excuse offered by the wealthy to deny services to the poor
—A Leftist's definition

Rather go to bed without dinner than to rise in debt.
—BENJAMIN FRANKLIN

Did you watch the Golden Globes? If you've got better things to do with your time, like most of us, here's the one-sentence version: It's one of a series of Hollywood parties in which all the celebrities pat themselves on the back for how talented they are. Almost always at these events some movie star who wins an award gets on stage and preaches about the need to help the poor or the less fortunate. Usually they blast evil Republicans in the process. Most of them are drunk when they do it. That's not a joke.

In 2015, for example, Moët & Chandon was named the official Champagne for the Golden Globes—yes, an "official Champagne"—and provided 400 magnums for the evening. A magnum of Champagne is the equivalent of two regular bottles. Stars were served 1,500 Moët Impérial minis on the red carpet; 500 cocktails at the bars, and the aforementioned 800 bottles, or 7,500 glasses, of Champagne at their tables during the ceremony.[1]

Look, I like to have a good time as much as anyone. And if

the people putting on the Golden Globes can afford to spend such ungodly sums on a bunch of pampered liberals, so be it. However, I don't need these same people, liquored up, caviar-stuffed, and driven around in limousines, to lecture us about how Republicans don't care about the poor. These people pour more money down their throats on a single night than many Americans earn in an entire year.

Of course, Leftists have never really cared about budgets or spending restraints or a sadly outdated concept like thrift. Their answer to every problem is to spend more money—more of regular Americans' tax dollars—on programs that don't work and problems they know they'll never be able to solve.

I could, of course, provide plenty of examples of this. Yet for the moment, let's just take one.

In 2009, the green-energy company Solyndra—which made solar panels—received a $535 million loan from the Obama administration. President Obama, who has supported any effort to send tax dollars to combat the menace of "global warming," praised the company as "leading the way toward a brighter and more prosperous future." Two years later the company went bankrupt, leaving the taxpayers to pay for its $535 million loan.[2] What became clear was that the company had misled the federal government from the beginning to secure the loan. What was worse, though, was that they had help on the inside. The Obama administration, to help political buddies championing Solyndra, cut corners to make the loan happen in the first place.[3]

Of course, $500 million is nothing to a federal government that is currently in debt to the tune of $19 trillion. And there are endless examples—in both parties, to be fair—of reckless runaway spending and enormous waste. Think of the infamous "Bridge to Nowhere"—a Republican-backed boondoggle that would have connected a small town in Alaska to an airport on an island of fifty people. The locals already have the option of using a ferry to get to the airport for a cost of all of $6, but they didn't want to wait for the ferry—sometimes the wait was as long as thirty whole minutes! So Alaska's representatives in Washington—Republicans—wanted the American taxpayer to foot the bill for a bridge, at a cost of $320 million. The Heritage Foundation listed the project as an expensive and unnecessary "embarrassment."[4]

It's not just politics—this free-spending attitude has taken over our culture. America's elite have adopted the conspicuous consumption of a Saudi royal family. Credit cards and readily available credit have destroyed the concept of frugality and purposeful spending—and destroyed plenty of families' bank accounts. The Left promises Americans that they can have everything whether or not they are actually able to afford any of it. "Life, Liberty the pursuit of Happiness," has morphed into "pursuit of a smart phone, an X-Box, a curved HDTV, a new car every couple of years," and on and on and on.

As a nation, we've forgotten what it means to live within our means. We've forgotten that a dollar spent by government is a dollar taken away from a family. On average, we are saving literally nothing for a rainy day,[5] with the expectation that someone will bail us out. We've forgotten the important role thrift played in our nation since its founding. We no longer teach the concept to children in school. It's high time we started to remember the meaning of the word—as one of our most famous Founding Fathers did.

A PENNY SAVED, A PENNY EARNED

Benjamin Franklin was one of America's most revered Founders, and his inspiring rags-to-riches story rightly earned him the title, "The First American." He preached frugality all of his life, though he was a man of extravagant tastes and habits. This is not necessarily a contradiction. Franklin was able to build a fortune because he recognized, as he famously put it, "a penny saved is a penny earned." When he was America's ambassador to France, and then England, he appeared before European aristocrats in a humble coonskin cap and met the bejeweled king of England in a plain brown suit.[6] He did this not because he was unable to afford jewels and silks and the other finery to which diplomats became accustomed—he was. He dressed in that simple style to prove a point: that America was different. Unlike Europeans, Americans did not have a desire to impress others through displays of excess and extravagance.

Franklin lived the value of thrift all of his life, as a poor man and as a rich man. Two years after he started a business he had paid off all of his debts through careful, simple living. Through this example, he encouraged Americans to understand the power that derives from making your own way, living carefully and within your means so you can build up your wealth and possessions, saving and sacrificing so you understand the value of owning something of your own. This was the true path to personal liberty. With Franklin's help, America in many ways created the concept of the self-made man—that you didn't become wealthy or successful solely by chance or because you happened to be born into a noble or royal class.

In his autobiography, Franklin published his thirteen virtues, his personal rules to live by. Among them was frugality: "make no expense but do good to others or yourself" (i.e., waste nothing). Franklin urged that citizens be not only frugal in possessions, but in words ("Speak not but what may benefit others or yourself"), appetite ("eat not to dullness; drink not to elevation"), and time management ("lose no time; be always employed in something useful; cut off all unnecessary actions").[7]

Other Founders shared those views. Though they understood public debt was sometimes a necessity, they lived in fear of the young republic living too far beyond its means. "There is not a more important and fundamental principle in legislation," James Madison said in a 1790 speech, "than that the ways and means ought always to face the public engagements; that our appropriations should ever go hand in hand with our promises."[8] As George Washington warned lawmakers in 1793, "No pecuniary consideration is more urgent, than the regular redemption and discharge of the public debt: on none can delay be more injurious, or an economy of time more valuable."[9]

I always admired Ben Franklin, and I've tried to follow his advice in my own life. It started when I was just a kid, growing up with a poor family in a tiny house in a neighborhood full of rich families and big houses. In those days, my hustle was landscaping. And it taught me the importance of thrift in ways I never forgot.

For a good eight years or so, I spent every Saturday and Sunday in the summertime mowing the lawns of my rich neighbors. It was hot, sweaty, hard work, but it was good money. I charged $5 per lawn, and $10 for a big one (but in this neighborhood, even the small yards were pretty big). On a given day, I could knock out six lawns. Of course, I didn't get started on Sundays until after mass at Queen of All Saints, and I had to work around baseball games, too. Whenever I could, though, I was out there with my dad's old Toro lawn mower cutting that grass, and I loved it. I loved the insanely gratifying feeling I got when I earned my own money.

I wasn't the only game in town. Some professional landscapers worked the neighborhood, too. I remember their big trucks that would drive by when they saw me out mowing, and the guys sitting across the front seat would give me the death glare. Who the heck was I, some kid, to move into their territory? Well, I was cheaper, for one, and I did a better job than they did. Sometimes the "pros" would be mowing a lawn next to me—all three of them working on one lawn—and I'd still finish mine before they did.

The thrill of beating the competition came in a close second to earning my own money. I was proud that because I worked faster, harder, and more carefully, I was the best mower around. And my neighbors knew it. I was never short of customers, despite the professional landscapers' best efforts. They used to mark the houses where I would work, and then they'd come around and try to convince the homeowner to give them a try, essentially trying to steal my customers. Sometimes it worked— for a time. The rich Sauganash families would try out the pros, but it didn't last long. After a week or two they dumped the landscaping crew and called me back.

My companion business in the Chicago winters was, of course, snow shoveling. Winters in Chicago were brutal, but very profitable. When the snow fell, I'd get out early in the morning and shovel snow until after dark. It was the hardest work I've ever done—far more physically demanding than mowing lawns. Chicago snow is wet and heavy, and usually fell with a wet layer that sank to the bottom. More snow would fall on top, and that made for twenty to thirty pounds per shovelful. And I went through about ten driveways a day. Snowblowers were useless—a Chicago snowfall would chew up a snowblower and spit it out. I could earn $10 for shoveling a driveway, and $15 for clearing the patio and sidewalks, too.

But even in the winters, I had to deal with the landscaper guys in their trucks. They would attach a snowplow to the front and get rid of the snow a lot faster than me. However, I was cheaper, and the real advantage was that I was more available. I would trudge through the heavy snowdrifts and start work right away, while it often took the truck a while to even get to me. Whenever I knocked on the rich folks' doors and asked if they wanted their walk shoveled, I never had anyone tell me, "No, thanks, I'll wait for the truck." When the truck finally did show up with its plow, there I would be, shoveling away, with a trail of clear walks and happy customers behind me.

One day, this fierce local competition with the landscapers taught me a lesson about thrift I've never forgotten. It was summer, and I was mowing a big lawn on Kirkpatrick Street, and my old friends in the landscaping truck pulled up to the house directly across the street from my job. The three guys got out, went to the back of their truck, and pulled out three lawn mowers. But these were different. In those days, the big, red, gas-guzzling Toros like my dad's were pretty much the only mowers anybody had. The mowers these guys brought out were brand-new looking, and green. "Lawn-Boy" was the brand.

Frankly, they didn't look like much. My Toro was bigger and tougher. Pushing it was a chore, but it got the job done. So I expected to easily cream the competition yet again. Nothing could beat me and my Toro.

So I kept at it, and everything was going fine, until I looked over after a little while and saw that the landscapers were nearly done! They and their Lawn-Boys were absolutely crushing me! They were going way faster than I was, and all I could do was watch in astonishment as they zipped over that neighboring lawn.

This would not stand. I didn't know what sort of tricks these guys had up their sleeves, but I was sure going to find out. That very evening, I came back from mowing and asked my dad to take me to the hardware store. I had to see what this was all about.

Sure enough, the salesman told us the newest thing in cutting lawns was the Lawn-Boy mower. It had a drivetrain with a fast and slow speed, and I had seen just how fast the fast speed went.

Immediately I knew what I had to do. If I was going to compete, if I was going to keep my business afloat, I had to upgrade my equipment. A Lawn-Boy cost around $140, which was a ton of money for a kid, but I did have some savings, after cutting a lot of lawns. I considered it, and realized the expense was worth it. I bought myself a Lawn-Boy.

It turned out to be the best investment I had ever made in my entire young life.

That Lawn-Boy mowed down those thick Chicago creeping bent grass blades like a hot knife slicing through butter. I was back in business, and faster than before. My customers were happy, and I was happy the money was rolling in again.

And it was only possible because I saved so much of my lawn-mowing money. Because I understood how important it was to be thrifty, to save for unexpected problems—like competitors trying to muscle you out with better equipment—I was able to save my business and keep the cash flow going.

If a young kid with a weekend lawn-care business can figure that out, shouldn't all those supposedly smart politicians in Washington be able to?

THE CRASS CLINTON MONEY GRAB

Clearly, I don't have any objection to making money—I've had the entrepreneurial bug since I was a kid. I don't fault anyone for the pursuit of wealth. One of the things many Americans like about Donald Trump is that he is unapologetic about being "really rich." As Donald points out many times, when you have enough money of your own, you don't have to answer to anybody.

It seems to me, though, that there are limits to what you need to do to make a buck. And some people, especially Leftist elites who love to lecture the rest of us, cross them all the time. Look no further than the obscene, shameful, unethical, and possibly illegal money grab that has been undertaken over the past few decades by those grotesque Gatsbys of greed and gluttony, Bill and Hillary Clinton.

After President Harry Truman left office in 1953, he lived on an army pension of $112.56 a month.[10] That year he reported $34,176.70 in income. In 1954 he earned $13,564.74.[11] Truman lived a modest life back home in Independence, Missouri, and, until he agreed to write his memoirs, he declined almost any offer to make money off of his service as President. He turned down $100,000 offers to sit on corporate boards.[12] He rejected $10,000 for a one-time TV appearance with his daughter.[13] This was a lot of money in those days. "I could never lend myself to any transaction, however respectable," Truman said, "that would commercialize on the prestige and dignity of the office of the presidency."[14]

Most of the country agreed with Truman's attitude, finding the idea of a former President making a fortune off of his public service unseemly. Even the much-beloved Ronald Reagan suffered from brutal criticism when, after leaving office, he accepted an offer to deliver a speech in Japan for $2 million.[15] Reagan was a modest man who did not live an extravagant lifestyle, and the criticism stung.

But compare these former Presidents to Bill Clinton, who made nearly $30 million from just two of his post-presidency books. Bill Clinton has had no compunction about making a dime from his time in public office; he has charged more than $100 million just for the speeches he's given alone.[16] And by a number of accounts, many of the recent speeches were little more than shakedowns of foreign governments wanting favors from his wife Hillary Clinton's State Department.

A blockbuster book, *Clinton Cash,* outlined a long list of the Clintons' efforts to pry a nickel out of every person they encountered even if it violated basic common sense, good taste, or propriety. Helpfully, *Breitbart News* put together a listing of the top allegations, all of which were reported by mainstream media publications.[17] Here are some of the best:

The New York Times: "Clinton Foundation Shook Down a Tiny Tsunami Relief Nonprofit for a $500,000 Speaking Fee"[18]

International Business Times: "Hillary Clinton's State Dept. Gave Clinton Foundation Donors Weapons Deals"[19]

The Washington Post: "Clintons Hid 1,100 Foreign Donor Names in Violation of Ethics Agreement with Obama Admin."[20]

Vox: "At Least 181 Clinton Foundation Donors Lobbied Hillary's State Dept."[21]

The New Yorker: "Bill Clinton Scored a $500,000 Speech in Moscow Paid for by a Kremlin-backed Bank"[22]

The Wall Street Journal: "Clinton Foundation Violated Mem-
orandum of Understanding with the Obama Admin. by
Keeping Secret a Foreign Donation of Two Million Shares
of Stock from a Foreign Executive with Business Before
Hillary's State Dept."[23]

The New York Times: "Hillary Clinton's Campaign Claims
She Had No Idea Her State Dept. Was Considering
Approving the Transfer of 20% of U.S. Uranium to the
Russian Govt.—Even as the Clinton Foundation Bagged
$145 Million in Donations from Investors in the Deal"[24, 25]

Bloomberg: "A For-Profit University Put Bill Clinton on Its
Payroll and Scored a Jump in Funding from Hillary
Clinton's State Dept. When *Clinton Cash* Revealed the
Scheme, Bill Clinton Quickly Resigned"[26]

The Washington Post: "Bill and Hillary Clinton Have Made
at Least $26 Million in Speaking Fees from Entities Who
Are Top Clinton Foundation Donors"[27]

Politico: "Hillary's Foundation Accepted $1 Million from
Human Rights Violator Morocco for a Lavish Event"[28]

In 2013 *The New York Times,* of all places, offered grotesque
and embarrassing details of Bill Clinton's quest to cash in on his
public service. He was invited to speak at the ninetieth birthday
party of his friend, fellow statesman, and Nobel Prize winner, the
former Israeli Prime Minister Shimon Peres. It's the kind of nice
gesture one former leader usually makes toward another—except
with the Clintons, there was a catch (there's always a catch): Bill
wanted $500,000 to show up and speak. What a mensch! Even
the liberal *New Yorker* magazine recently posed the question:
"How much more money does Bill Clinton need?"[29] Remember
Truman's vow not to "commercialize on the prestige and dignity
of the office of the presidency"? Clearly that means about as much
to Bill Clinton as being faithful to his wife.

These days Bill and Hillary are awash in an orgy of spending—

of course, maybe I shouldn't use the word "orgy" when discussing Bill Clinton—that they've made off of their time in public life. A lot of it has been wasted. *The New York Times* reported that the Clinton Foundation "ran multimillion-dollar deficits for several years, despite vast amounts of money flowing in."[30] Leaders of the Clinton Foundation fly employees around the world to gather "ideas" for various feel-good big-government schemes and then do nothing with them. Bill and Hillary have been known—for any number of reasons—to travel in separate jets to the same event (the story goes that Hillary's jet has about thirty seats—but Bill's has no seats, only beds). They pay for expensive reports from consulting groups and then ignore them.[31]

And it's still not enough. When Hillary announced she was running for President, a reporter asked Bill if he would keep giving speeches for money, since the invitations obviously could have conflicts of interest. "Oh, yeah," Bill replied. "I gotta pay our bills."[32] I guess lawyers and operatives and PR teams must be very expensive—which makes sense when you've got as much to hide as the Clintons do.

THE AGENDA BEHIND WASHINGTON'S SPENDING SPREE

We are spending ourselves into oblivion. Democrats and Republicans in Washington are out of control—and everyone knows it. In 2014 *The Daily Signal,* a publication of the Heritage Foundation, listed some of the "wackiest" examples of wasteful government spending. They included:

- $856,000 to teach mountain lions how to walk on treadmills, so they could study the animal's instincts.
- $387,000 to study the effects of Swedish massages on rabbits.

- $10,000 to monitor the growth rate of salt-marsh grass. Or, as *The Daily Signal* put it, "In other words, the government is paying people to watch grass grow."
- More than $200,000 to study how and why Wikipedia is sexist.
- $371,026 to study whether mothers love dogs as much as they love kids.[33]

Did I mention our national debt is $19,236,979,915,729 (that's 19 *trillion*)?

There's a reason why the Left wants to spend and spend and spend: It gives them power. Administering expensive programs and popular-sounding policies require staffs and bureaucracies and more and more tax dollars. Someone has to run the agencies that watch grass grow, right? Add in the lobbyists for corporations and special-interest groups who want government perks for their clients and you have a spending frenzy. Look at this chart for the Obama years:

Total public debt by month

In trillions of 2014 dollars. Non-adjusted dollar figures indicated with dashed lines.

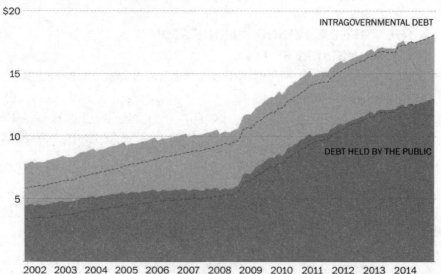

As Texas Senator Ted Cruz likes to point out, when President Obama took office, the federal debt was a little more than $10 trillion. Now it's over $19 trillion. "Just think about that for a moment," Cruz notes. "It took forty-three presidents nearly 220 years to accumulate $10 trillion in debt. . . . President Obama has doubled that."[34] It will take decades for our kids and grandkids to repay this.

But worse than Washington's chronic spending habit is that our leaders are actively encouraging the spend, spend, spend mentality throughout our society. Ever heard the expression "save for a rainy day"?

Too many Americans don't think they will ever have rainy days. We save far less, on average, than citizens in other places with first-world economies. In 2005, the average U.S. savings rate was 1.5 percent. By 2013, the rate was 2.6 percent. By contrast, the savings rate in Sweden was 10 percent, Germany was 10.5 percent, and France was 12.3 percent.[35]

According to one site that examines Americans' debt rate, the average U.S. household with debt carries an average total debt of $129,579.[36] The average credit card debt is over $15,000. The average auto loan is around $26,000 and the average student loan debt is nearly $48,000.[37]

Washington doesn't encourage us to change those habits; instead it promises to bail people out.

For decades, administrations from both parties encourage every American to own a home as "the American dream." And that is the American Dream—if you can afford it. However, Washington wanted people to get the dream on the cheap and encouraged banks to give interest-only loans to people who couldn't afford them. Then when the major Wall Street banks started to fail because of these bad loans, the government bailed them out. And they bailed out homeowners, too.

When General Motors began to teeter toward bankruptcy, due to decades of bad decisions, a greedy autoworkers union, and cars nobody wanted, government jumped in and bailed GM out, too. And I'm sure it was just a coincidence that GM is riddled with union influence. When the United Auto Workers union wants a bailout for their people, Democrats jump, afraid of losing their union cash. The folks at Lehman Brothers didn't have a union—that's not how they do business. I guess that was just too bad for them. If you want free money from the Obama administration, all you have to do is call your friendly local union boss.

Now Hillary Clinton wants to spend $350 billion to eliminate college debt.

"No family and no student should have to borrow to pay tuition at a public college or university."[38] That sure sounds nice—but guess who has to pay for that? Not the Clintons (though before long they'd probably be able to afford it). No, you will pay for it. You will pay for kids who probably shouldn't go to college in the first place. We need plumbers and carpenters and janitors, too—trades that require certain skills, but not necessarily a college degree. And frankly, it's not always worth it to sit around somewhere for four years listening to beatnik professors and writing haikus about corporate greed. If some parent wants to pay for their kid to waste their time like that, fine. But not on my dime. No, sir.

Of course Bernie Sanders went even further in 2016—calling for a free government-run health-care program for every single American and illegal immigrant, tuition-free schools, paid family and medical leave for all workers, jobs for disadvantaged youth regardless of qualifications or need, and universal child care and pre-kindergarten. *The Wall Street Journal* estimated that his proposal would cost $19 trillion—doubling the size of our already massive federal debt—and in the process vastly expand the federal government.[39] This of course is what the Left wants all along. We will all be hostages to the state because we wouldn't have much money to subsist on our own. At least Sanders is (somewhat) honest about it—he wants to tax Americans to oblivion to pay for free stuff for a lot of people who don't de-serve it.

RETURN TO SANITY

Rescuing the concept of thrift is essential to stopping the Left's march to a socialist utopia. And the first way to do that is at home with our kids. We don't have to give our children every new trendy object they see on TV. We can give them allow-ances and require them to restrain their spending based on what they've earned. I fear this is an increasingly old-fashioned idea these days. Also important is the concept of investment—putting money away and watching it grow, or using it to buy something that will make you *more* money like a new lawn mower—as op-posed to busting open a piggy bank whenever a new Star Wars Lego set comes out. Parents also should keep a closer eye on their kids and video games. With even young kids being automati-cally more tech-savvy than their parents, there's all kinds of new mischief for them to get into. In 2014, Google was forced to refund $15 million to parents from their children who pur-chased apps without permission.[40] Apple was ordered to pay at least $32.5 million.[41]

And, of course, we need to put into power in Washington people who understand the meaning of the phrase "fiscal disci-pline." When Ted Cruz tried to force the Obama administra-tion to support deep spending cuts in return for passing an increase in our debt limit, he was attacked. *By Republicans.* Vi-ciously attacked in editorial pages and various news articles for being reckless. He wasn't the one being reckless; the Obama ad-ministration was! It's an insane world where up is down and right is wrong.

The entrenched interests in Washington will do anything to keep the cash flowing. As Senator Rand Paul is fond of explain-ing, the reason we're in this mess is that when both sides get together, they always seem to agree on raising spending. Senator Paul calls it an "unholy alliance." When one side wants to spend money on something, they start bargaining and before you know it, spending and debt climb even higher.

Want to find out who's footing the bill? It's a one-step process. All you have to do is look in the nearest mirror.

5. INDIVIDUALITY

noun in·di·vid·u·al·i·ty   \in-də-vi-jə-'wa-lə-tē\

(1.) the quality that makes one person or thing different from all others
—Merriam-Webster's definition

(1.) dangerous deviation from approved standards and viewpoints

(2.) a form of selfishness and self-centeredness that must be stamped out in order to create the emergence of a collective identity
—A Leftist's definition

The creatures outside looked from pig to man, and from man to pig, and from pig to man again; but already it was impossible to say which was which.

—GEORGE ORWELL, *ANIMAL FARM*

Think of your average Sunday. Maybe you have eggs and bacon for breakfast. Maybe you go to church. Maybe you pick up a Big Gulp on your way home to watch football. And during commercials, you flip back and forth between the game and the latest headlines from Fox News.

Here's what's interesting about all of that. Somewhere out there is a liberal trying to ban every one of these activities, in some form or another.

The World Health Organization and various Left-wing governments are launching a war on bacon.[1]

The ACLU likes to regulate our ability to worship and express our faith.

Do-gooders like Michael Bloomberg, the former mayor of New York, have tried to ban large sodas.

Leftist outlets like *Salon* have called for a "war on football."[2]

And, no surprise, the Left would love to get rid of conservative media under legislation in Congress with the Orwellian name "the Fairness Doctrine."[3]

Don't like any of that? Well, expressing your opinion against the deeply held views of the politically correct Left—"patriotic dissent" is what they called such views in the days of the George W. Bush presidency—might one day be illegal, too. At Yale University in 2015, some of the allegedly smartest kids in America willingly signed a petition to repeal the First Amendment.[4]

All of this, of course, is being done for our own good. We need to be controlled, regulated, babysat, told what to do. Anyone deviating from these positions—or offering their own views—is a threat to the collective. Such people therefore need to be neutralized. Individuality and individualism need to be suppressed, linked with selfishness, and reprogrammed out of every right-thinking American adult.

Liberals really, really, *really* like to talk about how open-minded they are—a lot. And yet, today, there are few doing more to suppress the individual's freedom to act, think, say, and write what they want in the United States than so-called progressives. All done in the name of "equality" and "fairness" and "the community." Nothing says open-minded like the way the emerging tin-pot totalitarians of the so-called progressive Left have stamped out politically incorrect views in the boardrooms of corporate America, in the classrooms of academia, and in a media culture that perpetuates an army of bloggers and second-rate "watchdogs" that cry racism and insensitivity the moment you deviate from the liberal Left narrative.

Liberals are masters of language control. The current attack on individualism has everything to do with a decades-long effort on behalf of radical Leftists and academics to impose so-called political correctness on the general public. The very term sends shivers down my back. Nothing "political" can be inherently "correct." Politics is by nature about opinions and points of view. You can oppose these opinions, but labeling them "incorrect" (another way of saying "unacceptable") digs at the very heart of the individual right to free speech embedded in our Constitution.

Examples of this plague on our freedom abound. We see it in Congress and agencies like the Federal Election Commission (FEC) and Federal Communications Commission (FCC). We see it in academia, where students and faculty alike don't just disagree with conservative positions, but effectively ban them from campus. And we see it in the media, where liberal bias is rampant, and positions outside the media's own Lefty-fantasy "mainstream" (i.e., conservative positions) are either given short shrift or are pilloried outright.

From the corrupting halls of Congress to the ivy-covered walls of our colleges and universities to the quickly emptying newsrooms of the mainstream media, a chilling conformity—a new orthodoxy of thought—is settling in. The "open-minded" liberals of this country sure are doing a lot to close the minds— and mouths and keyboards—of those who disagree with them.

In fact, today, Americans are being actively encouraged to disdain individualism in favor of a creeping collectivism that will ultimately take the fight out of America by neutering our capacity for individual endeavor. In order to achieve this collectivism, as any politburo member in good standing could tell you, you must control what the people hear, think, and say. And the only way to do that is to be relentless in indoctrinating the populace with constant propaganda spouting the pieties of the new, blatantly collectivist, militantly multiculturalist, and radically antitraditionalist worldview—and to convince this same populace to rat out anyone who doesn't agree with Big Brother.

Free thought is becoming more and more unwelcome, and those who dare to break with the new orthodoxy must undergo

Maoist-like "recrimination" sessions or suffer severe financial and personal consequences. Just ask Brendan Eich, the creator of JavaScript and cofounder of Mozilla, who was hounded out as that organization's CEO in 2014 because he once—six years earlier—made a donation in favor of California's Proposition 8, which stated that "only marriage between a man and a woman is valid or recognized in California."[5]

The PC culture has even taken over comedy; having a sense of humor is nearly outlawed. Liberals are so sensitive—and their fervently held beliefs so absolute—that they can't recognize a joke anymore. What would they make of Lenny Bruce or Richard Pryor in their heydays? Our country is standing on the edge of a very slippery slope, and the Left is poised with banana peels and nudges to make sure we go down it.

It's up to the rest of us to make sure as hell this doesn't happen.

I didn't rise from poverty because I was the smartest, handsomest, or most accomplished person in the world. I wasn't handpicked for greatness by the state. Like most everybody else who's accomplished anything in life, I did it because I wanted it more. From a young age, I knew what I wanted—and to get it, I knew I had to work harder and smarter than everybody else around me.

That was especially true in the New York commodities market. Trading pits are like snake pits—just slightly more dangerous. They are all about survival of the fittest. And the furthest from the fittest are the newest, least experienced traders. For these folks, at the very bottom of the food chain, there are only a few ways to move up. You can make some big trades on your own (which is tough, because you have to get people to notice you and trade with you), or you can go the less advisable route, and stake out your territory by standing up to one of the hotshot, big-time traders.

That was a choice I found myself faced with early on. I was trying to make a name for myself, but it was tough: I was one of the newest guys in the pit. I didn't have any winning track record. I might as well have been invisible, just another body taking up space and consuming precious oxygen on the trading floor. One day, we found ourselves in a real frenzy—oil was spiking, and all seven or eight hundred of us in the pit were yelling over one another, climbing literally over each other's shoulders trying to make a trade. As sometimes happened, someone tripped, took another person with them, then another and another. Before we knew it, about eighty of us had crashed to the floor, including me. I looked up, and there, standing over me laughing, was a trader I'll call Hank.

Hank was one of the all-around biggest guys in the pit. He was huge, he slung big trades, and had a big ego to match. Nobody liked him, but because of his size and reputation, people just left him alone. Nobody ever stood up to him. And there he was, standing over me, laughing his obnoxious head off.

That was when I made my decision—one that probably a thousand other guys in my exact same position would *not* have made. I decided this was my moment. So I sprang up from the floor and charged at Hank. I grabbed him, and using my momentum and the fact he was taken completely by surprise, pushed him back several steps and then threw him bodily out of the trading pit. We ended up in a brawl—a fistfight on the floor of the New York Mercantile Exchange—before the security officers split us up.

My mother might not have thought of that as one of my proudest moments, but I had taken on a really big fish and lived to talk about it. I don't know which of us had bigger bruises from the scuffle, but it didn't matter. I was noticed. That's what really mattered. That's what made the difference.

I was fined $5,000 and suspended from trading for three days. But after I came back, I noticed more and more people coming to me to make trades. I had more respect from the other traders now, even from Hank. I had put myself on the map. That $5,000 fine eventually seemed like one of the best business expenses I ever paid.

I learned a valuable lesson from my scuffle with Hank, too: to make a place for yourself, you have to be tough, take risks, and be willing to piss some people off. You need to chart your own path as an individual. Don't be afraid of breaking away from the pack, even if you might end up looking like an idiot or losing what you've worked to achieve. Sadly, that's exactly the opposite of what we teach people, including our children, today. Now we tell them "everybody wins!" In youth sports these days, they give out trophies to everybody. In the real world, though, only the winners get the trophies. What happens when these kids wake up fresh out of college and realize they have to fight for themselves?

How did we get here from such noble, individualist beginnings? A conspiracy of Leftists in politics, academia, and the media have spent decades brainwashing our kids. It's going to take time, but we can fight and win back our country for sanity, honor, and individual freedom. We can start by teaching our kids about the true nature of our nation's beginnings, about a nation that was built by a people who fled the oppression of Europe to practice their faiths as their individual consciences demanded.

A NATION OF MAVERICKS

If you travel the world and ask people from other countries the first word that comes to their minds when you say, "America," I'd bet good money that a fair portion of them would say: "cowboy." And, despite the fact that the day of the cowboy is long gone, we should be proud of that word. Foreigners continue to associate America with cowboys because we still embody the individualistic grittiness of these wandering mavericks: We are loners, risk-takers, dreamers, and tough guys ready to get to work, get things done, and carve out a place in the world for ourselves.

America used to be the kind of place where you could do your own thing, even if it seemed odd or eccentric. A young Bill Gates spent his time tinkering with computers when hardly anybody knew what they were, and look what came from that. Who knows why people do what they do? I had a fairly unusual habit for a number of years; I used to fast every Tuesday. I did it for my mother. She was stricken with ovarian cancer, which spread quickly to her peritoneal region—that is, the lining along her stomach. I absolutely adored my mother, and it crushed me to watch her suffer through this disease. She went in for chemo-therapy every Tuesday, and whenever I could, I would go with her. The chemo would make her so nauseous that she couldn't eat, so on Tuesdays, I decided not to eat, either. I kept up that practice in her memory even after she passed away. Maybe people thought it was strange—here I was, a former pro athlete who tries to keep in good shape, refusing food one day a week. I didn't care. It was my way of honoring Mom.

One Tuesday in 2015, I found myself getting light-headed during a segment on the air. Soon I was breaking out in a sweat, and I knew something was going on. I decided to finally stop my Tuesday fast—maybe I was getting too old for it. Yet for many years, that was my habit and I stuck to it. Grieving is one of the most personal processes we can go through, and that was how I chose to do it. How I chose to honor my mom was some-thing that made me different—something that made me an individual.

Sadly, though, we are rapidly losing this sense of individual-ism in the United States. With the Bloombergs of the world in government telling you what you can and can't eat and drink, is it that hard to imagine that deciding to fast one day a week might one day be viewed as a "seditious" eating habit? It's hap-pening across our whole culture. Yesterday's cowboy is today's company man or conformist university professor—risk-averse, susceptible to groupthink, always needing direction and approval from an apparatchik above him. Asking for a place in the world instead of going out and taking it, even if it means losing your shirt (and everything else) a time or two before you get it right. We're going soft, and it isn't pretty.

Like capitalism, democracy is based on certain essential truths: Human beings have a natural right to be free; they are also self-interested, and that isn't going to change anytime soon. To govern a free people, a system must allow the power of self-interest to create mutually beneficial interactions that both generate and maintain freedom in a just society.

This is exactly the kind of society our Founding Fathers set out to create in the 1770s and 1780s. Yet our individualist roots go even deeper than the Revolution. We literally have individualism in our DNA. Nearly everyone in America is the descendent of risk-takers who came to these shores to carve out a new life for themselves, or the descendants of slaves who had to fight for centuries to get the legal and social recognition as individuals that is their natural right. We're a rough-and-tumble group of brawlers.

At least we used to be. After suffering under the tyranny of the British Crown and Parliament, a handful of brave souls—they faced certain death if captured—started a movement that spread across the thirteen original colonies and captured the hearts, minds, and souls of their countrymen.

What the United States did in the Revolutionary War and after is nothing short of a miracle. Not only did we defeat what was then the most powerful empire on earth, we went on to deliberately form a democratic form of republican government. The elites of the time—especially George Washington—turned their backs on millennia of precedent and, instead of creating a new monarchy and nobility with themselves at the helm, devised a government of, for, and by the people. It was a rebellion against the collectivism and groupthink that had lasted for centuries—the idea of the "divine right" of kings and queens to rule their people without their consent. The courage—the cojones, really—it took for these men to take up arms and risk everything to overturn their rulers is nothing short of astounding when you think about it.

Today, we take this for granted. The American Revolution

started what would be a wave of revolutions and peaceful tran-
sitions to one form of democracy or another over the next two
centuries. It was truly, profoundly shocking in its time. It was
so shocking, in fact, that when famed American painter Benjamin West told King George III that General Washington planned
to resign his position after the war, return to his farm, and not
seek permanent power (which he almost certainly could have
attained), the astonished monarch said: "If he does that, he will
be the greatest man in the world."[6] Washington was.

George Washington was a stunning example of individualist
fortitude and character in our Founding Fathers, but this deep
character and strength ran through the ranks of the Continental
Army and through the hearts of all true patriots. Their ancestors
had risked death, disease, bodily harm, homesickness, and virtual
exile. So that they could have the freedom to worship, trade,
and live as they pleased. So that the individual could triumph
over the collective. So that a man would be free from the coer-
cive power of the collective as long as he harmed no one else or
their property.

These were the men and women who made America. Of
course, not everyone was officially included in "the people" at the
time. Yet as a democratic republic, we've continued to evolve,
grow, and expand our understanding of freedom as essential to all
humans, regardless of race, gender, or religion. All this progress,
however, is denied by the progressives of today. They've come to
hate America so much that they don't even recognize the revolutionary character, individual strength, and preeminent historical
role our nation has played in creating, spreading, and maintaining
freedom in the world.

Just look at the history of the twentieth century: Liberals seem
to forget that the worst crimes of modern history—the Holo-
caust; the tens of millions killed, starved, or worked to death in
the USSR and China; the "Killing Fields" of Cambodia, to
name just a few—were all carried out in the name of one collectivist fantasy or another. Individualism is the direct opponent

of tyranny. Today's radical Leftists only care about individual liberty in the bedroom. They say they believe in "fairness" and "equality," but only on their terms.

How? Because both of these concepts are completely subjective. Who decides what is "fair" or "equal"? The only way to make things "fair" for everyone is to give someone or some group absolute power, and then impose this "fairness" on the rest of us. And you know what? We've already had a system like that in history—it's called communism, and, according to the landmark 1997 tome *The Black Book of Communism,* it was responsible for nearly 100 million deaths (plus all those who have been killed in collectivist paradises like China, Cuba, North Korea, and Vietnam in the decade since the *Black Book* was published).[7]

The genius of the American system—of the Founders—is that it does not make such value judgments, and therefore does not need such arbiters, who inevitably become one form of tyrant or another. These decisions—though I hesitate to even call them that—are instead guided by economist Adam Smith's "invisible hand" of the market, which creates efficiencies, drives innovation, incentivizes hard work, and generates wealth for anyone tough enough—and willing to work hard enough—to go out there, put something of their own or themselves at risk, and get something out of it. The genius of this market is enlightened self-interest. The decisions of millions of individuals cause goods and services to move around in the fairest way possible, at prices not determined by some politburo or government committee, but by what consumers are willing to pay. In other words, it's the simple law of supply and demand.

Unlike our friends in Europe, the United States has always taken the individualist path. However, today we're reversing course, and headed toward European-style paternalism. If we're not careful—if we don't start electing people who value individual freedom and recognize the dangers of collectivism—we could end up looking and feeling like a really, really big Sweden (or worse) before we know it.

The United States has never been a collectivist country, and we must never allow it to become one. America is a nation of mavericks, not sheep. Our founding was defined by breaking the rules, tearing ourselves away from the colonial power of Great Britain, and forging a new country out of a vast wilderness. This could not have been pulled off by people who valued cookie-cutter conformism. Our Founders understood, like many Americans understand today, that bucking tradition is sometimes the only way to get things done.

CONTROLLING WHAT YOU SAY

The threat to individuality and individualism isn't just theoretical. The attack has been mounting for decades. If you haven't heard about it, that's because the Left's accomplices in the media aren't willing to cover it. Washington Democrats, of course, are doing more than their share to restrict our speech and diminish individualism. They don't come right out and say that. Ever crafty, they use buzzwords like "campaign finance reform" and "money in politics" to mask their true intention: control political speech in this country so that all messages conform to their new rules—and help Democrats and their RINO (Republican In Name Only) enablers get elected.

Take, for example, the Democrats' shrill response to the Supreme Court's repeated decisions in recent years to protect First Amendment rights in regards to political speech—especially the *Citizens United v. Federal Election Commission* case. Again and again, Democrats make the argument that campaign contributions do not constitute political speech—as if giving money to a cause or candidate isn't by its very nature the making of a statement. And what is a statement? A form of speech! Not to mention the fact that, in today's world, you cannot effectively express an opinion without on some level spending money. "Campaign finance reform" is a farce.

Facing a Supreme Court that is actually defending the

Constitution (at least on this issue), Democrats have tried to make an end run around the Court by changing the Constitution itself. In the summer of 2014, then-Senate Majority Leader Harry Reid (D-NV), Senator Chuck Schumer (D-NY), and other members of the Democratic brain trust introduced a measure to amend the First Amendment as follows:

> Authorizes Congress and the states to regulate and set reasonable limits on the raising and spending of money by candidates and others to influence elections.
> Grants Congress and the states the power to implement and enforce this amendment by appropriate legislation, and to distinguish between natural persons and corporations or other artificial entities created by law, including by prohibiting such entities from spending money to influence elections.
> Declares that nothing in this amendment shall be construed to grant Congress or the states the power to abridge the freedom of the press.[8]

So, let me get this straight: The amendment would allow politicians in Washington, D.C., and state capitals to regulate speech that directly relates to the business of government and their jobs—the type of speech that should be most protected! This con job was nothing but a power grab to control how citizens—including corporations and conservative interest groups—can express their political views, a grab to help keep corrupt incumbents in office. After all, it's tough to be voted out of office when you help control what your opponents and constituents can say about you. And it's awfully hard to express one's individual right to a fair vote when the outcome of an election is effectively rigged.

Note the special carveout for the media. Reid and company were trying to make it so corporations and conservative interest groups would be muzzled, but unions and the Democrats' tame press would be free to spew any kind of biased crap they like. If they can't win elections fair and square, Democrats are more than willing to silence huge portions of the citizenry to stay in power. Had the amendment somehow passed, it would have been the first time one of the Constitution's core individual rights would have been infringed through the amendment process itself.[9] The attempt itself is disgraceful.

Thankfully, this amendment quickly died the death it deserved. But not without Democrats using it for their usual lies and demagoguery. Sadly, there are many more examples of this appalling behavior.

People, this is scary, scary stuff. In government, Democrats are using the levers of power to undermine our fundamental right to free speech. In a democratic republic like ours, without a free, fair choice in elections, individualism takes a back seat to collectivism.

Elsewhere in our society, liberals are policing thought and speech alike in a ludicrous effort to protect people from ideas and words that might offend them. We're on the fast track to serfdom, and half the country not only doesn't realize it, they are smiling as they are shackled.

CONTROLLING WHAT YOU THINK

The American university tradition is deeply enmeshed with the Enlightenment—the reason-based philosophical approach that had its beginnings in seventeenth-century Europe and saw its heyday in the eighteenth century[10] (one could make the case that its apotheosis was the American Revolution—an entire nation built on such core Enlightenment principles as rationality, liberty, and free thought).

Liberalism itself has its roots also planted deep in the Enlightenment. However, somewhere along the way—somewhere between Thomas Jefferson and Barack Obama—liberalism became completely unmoored from its Enlightenment roots.

Where once was reason, now the Left embraces irrationalism. Where once liberty was the goal, today liberalism is a force for conformity and oppression. Where once the individual was paramount, today's liberalism has become mired in collectivist claptrap. Where once free thought was the benchmark, for today's liberals, it's an obstacle—an enemy to be vanquished instead of a principle to be defended.

Nowhere is this more apparent—nowhere is American individualism more profoundly threatened—than in that deepest well of politically correct stupidity that is today's college or university campus. In fact, nowhere in our society today is the radical collectivist agenda more apparent than in places of "higher" learning.

For decades, college professors and administrators have done everything in their power to get rid of conservative voices on campus, whether in the faculty, student body, or campus groups. In today's campus atmosphere, holding conservative views is reflexively labeled as hateful, bigoted, or intolerant. Yet now, the beast created by these professors and administrators is turning on these institutions themselves. While most of the student protests over the last year or so have been frivolous at best, these colleges and universities deserve every moment of misery they get for churning out generations of liberal automatons ready to impose the new thought control on our country.

We all know that there is no quicker way to get someone to shut up in today's America than to call them a racist, sexist, homophobe, etc. By claiming (and teaching) that holding conservative positions is all these things and more—morally bankrupt, bad for society, and (always) the product of some kind of societal bias—campus liberals have been effective at shutting down the free exchange of ideas in the very institutions where such exchange should be encouraged. Conservative thought and individuals are not welcome on today's college campuses—period.

The events at uber-liberal Brown University late last year perfectly encapsulate the state of American academia, and the threat to individualism we face as a larger society. After a variety of racial controversies on campus, in November 2015 the school's President Christina Paxson made public a draft proposal to deal with supposed racial bias on Brown's campus—*Pathways to Diversity and Inclusion Plan: An Action Plan for Brown University*—which reads like a liberal-multicultural handbook and proposes allocating a staggering $100 million to "confront the issues of racism, power, privilege, inequity and injustice" at Brown.[11]

Did this satisfy the radical students? Of course not. These are children, being taught primarily by childish grown-ups, screaming about injustice while in one of the tallest, shiniest ivory towers in academia. And the few brave souls who dared to point out that conservatives and conservative views regularly face bias and discrimination at Brown? Suffice it to say, Brown will remain an "unsafe space" for those opposed to kneejerk liberalism for the foreseeable future.

I would like to point out, however, that during one of the various fracases engineered by radical students in which they directly confronted Paxson, Brown's president said something truly shocking for the sitting head of a modern Ivy League school: "Valuing people and agreeing with everything they demand are not the same thing."[12] While this is just plain common sense to most of us, this should be considered courageous and wise in the Ivy League context. In essence, Paxson directly contradicted one of the primary tenets of the new PC campus code. Will she face the vocational firing squad, too?

The situation at Brown and college campuses around the country should worry all Americans, even if you disagree with the conservative positions that are being banned by these self-appointed thought police. Barring actual libel, we should not be telling students or the American people what they can and cannot think. If we want free-thinking leaders—instead of coddled, conformist weaklings—in the coming generations, we need to stop treating them like Fabergé eggs and make them compete fairly in the marketplace of ideas.

The state of the First Amendment on college campuses has come to this: Many institutions have instituted "free speech zones" where students can—theoretically—go to speak their minds without backlash. Is it just me, or is this exactly backward? All parts of all colleges and universities should be "free speech zones." That the rest of these campuses are, effectively "anti-free-speech zones" is chilling.

American academia, though, is reaping what it has sowed. From places designed expressly for the free exchange of ideas, today's colleges and universities have become straitjackets of collectivist thought. The individual means nothing. Remember all those protesters and bumper stickers proclaiming during the George W. Bush administration that "Dissent Is Patriotic"? Turns out it's only patriotic if it's liberals dissenting against a conservative in power. The other way around? Racism, xenophobia, bigotry, and general stupidity.

A 2014 report by the Foundation for Individual Rights in Education, for example, found that nearly 60 percent of higher-education institutions in this country have policies infringing on First Amendment rights.[13] For decades, college and university faculty and administrations have worked to turn America's youth into radical Leftists—and now the Leftist beast is devouring itself. While I'm horrified by the direction of higher education in this country, I can't help laughing a little as I watch university and college administrators and faculty squirm as they try and handle the very kind of "dissent" they have so long supported. They haven't had to face anything like this for decades; academia has been one big "safe place"—as long as your views are liberal. Now the students have turned on their masters, literally.

But this is no laughing matter. Despite the turmoil on today's campuses, the trend in academia is ever Leftward. I have zero hope that those who lead our top institutions will really fight the Big Brother approach to college academics. Without free thought, there can be no individualism. Without real free thought at real universities, the individual will continue to take second place to the collective in the U.S. political discourse, as millions more indoctrinated liberals are thrust upon our economy.

CONTROLLING WHAT YOU HEAR

Then, of course, we have the media—perhaps the biggest culprit in the sad story of subverting the individual to the collective. Instead of Edward R. Murrow speaking truth to power during the McCarthy Era, we have Rachel Maddow regurgitating the lies of the powerful Leftist elite, denigrating American individualism, and celebrating collectivism (among many other "-isms"). I'd like to say American journalism is at its pathetic, juvenile nadir today, but I fear things are only going to get worse—for journalism, but also for America in general, and the individualistic nature that for centuries has driven our republic to success.

Of course, unofficial liberal media bias runs rampant, but plenty of today's media is proudly, openly biased in favor of "progressivism" and the Democratic Party. Even when trying to be fair, today's media almost always supports the establishment message: more government controlling more aspects of our lives from an ever-more centralized control center called Washington, D.C.

Even their media colleagues are calling them out on it. Take a look at these quotes gathered by the invaluable Media Research Center[14] website:

> *There is no doubt that the press failed to scrutinize this program [Obamacare] at the time of passage and during the context of the President's re-election. I think any reporter who would argue otherwise would be putting their head in the sand.*
> —*TIME*/MSNBC POLITICAL ANALYST MARK HALPERIN
> ON FOX NEWS CHANNEL'S *THE O'REILLY FACTOR*,
> NOVEMBER 21, 2013

*You know, it's fairly well discussed inside CBS News that there
are some managers recently who have been so ideologically
entrenched that there is a feeling and discussion that some of
them . . . have a difficult time viewing a story that may reflect
negatively upon government or the administration as a story of
value . . . They never mind the stories that seem to, for
example—and I did plenty of them—go against the grain of
the Republican Party . . . I didn't sense any resistance in
doing stories that were perceived to be negative to the Bush
administration—by anybody, ever. I have done stories that I
perceived were not received well because people thought they
would reflect poorly upon this [the Obama] administration.*

—FORMER CBS NEWS INVESTIGATIVE
CORRESPONDENT SHARYL ATTKISSON ON CNN'S
RELIABLE SOURCES, APRIL 20, 2014

The above quotes, my friends, are examples of the "neutral" mainstream media at work. Convinced in their own liberal colleges and universities—and reinforced by the echo chamber of their professional choices—today's mainstream media is a multibillion-dollar industry focused on the destruction of individual rights in favor of collectivist communes in the sky.

My colleagues at Fox strive to stay fair and balanced, and there are a few exceptions elsewhere in the media. Mark Halperin, quoted above, can often be relied on to tell it like it is and give us a peek behind the D.C. establishment's curtain. Over at CNN, Don Lemon is good at asking tough questions to people on all sides of an issue. And former *Tonight Show* host Jay Leno was typically an equal-opportunity jokester, skewering the Left *and* the Right in contrast to most of his late-night colleagues. Across most of the mainstream media, however, the message is clear: toe the liberal line or get the heck out.

And don't expect much to change anytime soon. These former gatekeepers of opinion live in a mind-numbing bubble in which they still think they set public attitudes. In the digital age, though, that is no longer the case. These types will keep chugging along until the writing is on the wall—or the pink slips have finally fully engulfed America's newsrooms.

Meanwhile the Left continues to seek ways to silence media outlets that don't follow the party line. Take, for example, the "Fairness Doctrine," which Democrats tried to revive in new form in 2014 via the Federal Communications Commission's "Multi-Market Study of Critical Information Needs," or "CIN" for short.

At the time, Republican FCC Commissioner Ajit Pai called out his colleagues in spectacular fashion on this issue in *The Wall Street Journal*:

> The purpose of the CIN, according to the FCC, is to ferret out information from television and radio broadcasters about "the process by which stories are selected" and how often stations cover "critical information needs," along with "perceived station bias" and "perceived responsiveness to underserved populations."[15]

Let's take one guess what types of media outlets the FCC would have targeted for "perceived station bias"? A liberal front group called Citizens for Responsibility and Ethics (CREW) actually sent a letter to the head of the FCC asking for Fox's broadcast licenses to be revoked.[16]

Do we have any other examples of the Obama administration using a supposedly neutral government agency to go after its critics and political opponents? That's right: President Obama's Internal Revenue Service (IRS) has clearly gone after groups that worked against the administration's agenda—and individuals, too! I myself got an audit in 2011, which I'm sure had nothing at all to do with my frequent statements on television opposing President Obama's reelection.

DIVERSE CONFORMITY

It's strange. While celebrating their very narrow definition of "diversity," the Left is also trying to force everyone to conform to an exact set of ethical and philosophical standards: to be the same. They are the ultimate conformists. They don't say that—they call it "equality" and "fairness"—but it comes down to the same thing: The Left wants a society where there are no losers in the game of life, a society without risk.

However, to be vibrant, dynamic, innovative, and strong, a society *must* have risk-takers, which means we must have both winners *and* losers. America has never rewarded winners and losers based on what's "fair." But that's happening more and more today, and as a result, we've become so coddled and afraid of risk that we've tried to make life free of all risk, for everyone, all the time. It's ridiculous.

At their core, Leftists—liberals, progressives, whatever—are collectivists. They believe that individuals should conform to the will of the whole, purportedly for the good of all. Yet as we've seen with depressing regularity in recent years, this drive toward collectivism is leading to a kind of thought tyranny we haven't dealt with in the country since the Red Scare days of the 1950s. All in the name of "fairness" and "equality," of course.

This collectivist approach to governing, though, comes at a very, very steep cost. Whether they admit it or not, the Left's obsessive drive for "fairness" for the collective is completely dependent on decreasing freedom for the individual. There simply is no other way to pursue the kind of society they want than tyranny. They may say they respect individual rights, but the policies they support suggest quite the opposite.

THE FIGHT CONTINUES

At the end of the day, liberals keep trying to make free people and free markets conform to their own arbitrary (and ultimately harmful) values. And it keeps not working out so great with consequences for all of us.

All human beings can and must be valued, but to say that everyone's work, education, knowledge, and capabilities are effectively "equal" or that we can somehow level the national playing field to be "fair" for everyone is absurd. The path of history is littered with the bodies of tens of millions of individuals sacrificed to the golden calf of the collective. We can't let it happen again.

We owe it to these tens of millions to keep up the fight against Leftist radicals and save this country from itself. The creeping collectivism of the postwar period became a tidal wave with Barack Obama's swearing-in as President in 2009. If we don't start really fighting back—and if we don't take back the White House and have to suffer under yet another collectivist President (not to mention the risk of having to deal with the Clintons again)—we're going to be in big, big trouble.

6. DOMINION

noun do-min-ion / dəˈminyən/

(1.) sovereignty; control
"man's attempt to establish dominion over nature"
                                          —Merriam-Webster's definition

*(1.) the dangerous belief that human beings matter more than
plants or animals, when in fact animals have as many rights as
people*
                                          —A Leftist's definition

*Then God said, "Let us make mankind in our image, in our
likeness, so that they may rule over the fish in the sea and the
birds in the sky, over the livestock and all the wild animals, and
over all the creatures that move along the ground." (Genesis
1:26)*

Millions of Americans are animal lovers—and I count myself
among them. One afternoon when I was a boy, a large Great
Dane–looking mutt wandered to our house and stayed. I loved
that dog immediately. My father, however, knowing this
dog must belong to a family that missed him, drove all around
the neighborhood trying to find his owner. We never found
him, so I got to keep him. His name was Duke and he was a
treasured pet.

As much as I loved Duke, I understood he was an animal and
that I was his owner. I thought his life was precious, but not
equally important as a human being's. Apparently, a growing
number of Americans believe otherwise.

In a 2015 Gallup poll, almost a third of Americans—32
percent—said they believe animals should be given the same

rights "to be free from harm and exploitation" as people.[1] I'm all for protecting animals from harm, but there's a limit.

The Left has become unhinged over its belief in the rights and privileges of animals, and plants, and the environment. And it's only getting worse because these ideas are making their way into the popular consciousness as a form of pet political correctness. For example, a new phrase—"pet parent"—has come into vogue, which creates in some people's minds the disturbing idea that dogs and cats are similar to children.[2] In fact, one (I hope) dubious survey found that 76 percent of dog owners preferred to be called "dog parents" or "pet parents."[3] That's a cute idea, I suppose, but it's not reality.

And yet "pet parent" is being attacked by Leftists because the term "pet" is insulting.[4] Insulting to whom, you ask? Why, to dogs, cats, and hamsters. Pets should instead be called "companion animals" and pet owners "human carers."[5] The term "wildlife" is also an insult—we should refer to goats, monkeys, slugs, snails, beavers, and wolverines as "free living."[6]

This is nothing compared to a new radical movement which has sprouted up—if you'll excuse the pun—that not only condemns the practice of using animals or animal by-products for food or clothing, but attacks humans for the "unnecessary" use of any living thing. It's called freeganism.

What is a freegan, you, a normal person, might ask?

Well, a freegan is one of a group of people who "employ alternative strategies for living based on limited participation in the conventional economy and minimal consumption of resources."[7] Freegans eat nothing that has to be killed or uprooted from the ground or collected from bushes or trees. They reject man's "exploitation" of animals and refuse use of any goods that include animal by-products. One of the things they advocate is dumpster diving (which they sometimes label under the less disgusting term "urban foraging"). In other words, they commend those who get their food, clothing, and other goods from the trash.[8] Let's hope they aren't feeding soiled garbage to their own babies. (*Side note*: Another of the freegan principles is "working less,"[9] but that's probably not a real surprise, is it?)

We've come to a crazy place: groups that bemoan the slaughter of cows, but have no problem with the annual slaughter of human embryos or viable fetuses; clueless elitists who give their fortunes to their cats upon their deaths, instead of to charities that help orphans and veterans and, you know, human beings. And the reason for this is the endless media campaigns of radical Leftist organizations that have a greater regard for animals than people. It's why the once obvious notion that man is superior to nature has been reversed and rejected.

Let me be clear: I believe humans should care for animals, and protect them from unnecessary cruelty. They are God's creatures, but they are not by any scope of the imagination our equals—or our betters. It's time we get this kooky Leftist idea out of everyone's heads for good.

HUMANISM: A DEFENSE

Let's start by defending a group of animals that radical Leftists have tried to turn into the world's villains. Humans.

For the past five hundred years or so, Western civilization has moved inexorably away from the Dark Ages and in the general direction of modernity. A lot of good things happened over that time. Some of those good things have been the result of inventions and scientific advancements. Yet just as many have been the result of evolving thought about humans and how we should interact with one another. This movement led away from cruel fiefdoms and total subjugation beneath kings and toward the notion that humans should be able to determine their own lives. The invention of the movable press allowed the mass production of books and pamphlets, which, in turn, led to greater enlightenment and debate. It forced people to confront other people with different ideas, without (always) trying to lop their heads off. Print led to the various revolutions, including the American Revolution, which put the finest point yet on the notion that humans are capable of self-determination and have been granted rights by God Himself to govern themselves. I haven't seen a cat accomplish any of this.

On a serious note, though, the Judeo-Christian faith upon which America is founded holds that, indeed, man is special in God's eyes. Our Declaration of Independence declares that our rights are guaranteed by "Nature's God," and every piece of our currency bears the official motto "In God We Trust." Man is not just another animal. Man has a soul and is capable of virtue and self-improvement. Now don't get me wrong, my dog is plenty virtuous, but his only attempts at self-improvement involve getting into the garbage and eating until he can't walk anymore. Obviously, part of that Judeo-Christian argument requires man to be a good steward of nature and animals, but also to have dominion, or control, over them:

> Then God said, "Let us make mankind in our image, in our likeness, so that they may rule over the fish in the sea and the birds in the sky, over the livestock and all the wild animals, and over all the creatures that move along the ground." (Genesis 1:26)

Since even before the earliest pioneer days, Americans have enjoyed—and bravely endured—a truly unique relationship with the earth and its creatures. Carved out of the last major unspoiled continent of wilderness on the planet, America is a product of man's relationship with untamed nature. It hasn't been an easy road.

Greeted at Jamestown by malarial mosquitoes, the first settlers had no idea what hit them or how they had contracted such virulent illness. "Our men were destroyed with cruell diseases as Swellings, Flixes, Burning Fevers, and by warres, and some departed suddenly, but for the most part they died of meere fam-

ine," observed English nobleman George Percy, one of the few
who miraculously lived through it all.[10]

Historians now believe that the disease Percy described was
most certainly malaria. And if colonists were mystified by the
disease itself, their remedies were borderline comical. They
bathed their legs in hot milk and drank horrid concoctions
brewed from local plants. Or, as one recommendation went:
"A spider bruised in a cloth, spread upon linnen and applied to
the forehead or temples." Only a third of the original Jamestown colonists survived the first year.

After that, things improved for America's earliest surviving
settlement, but only marginally. Diseases Europeans had never
dreamed of in their wildest nightmares ravaged their ranks.
Swarms of insects nearly carried them off. And plagues of deadly
snakes, spiders, and other unimaginable creatures must have persuaded some that they had taken a wrong turn along the way
and had landed in the depths of hell. Yet they stuck with it. Visions
of freedom and prosperity urged them inland and pressed them
westward.

Over the generations, colonists marched west into hostile
territory. Ferocious wild animals patrolled the frontier, raided
human encampments, devoured small children. Entire families
survived with nothing more than the tools they carried with
them. Can you imagine what it must have been like to hike the
family across the Appalachian Mountain range in the dead
of winter with just a horse and wagon? Imagine the terror that
must have been inspired by the summer electrical storms in the
American Midwest. Or the first tornadoes? Or crossing the Mis-
sissippi River and the endless plains? And, yet, they pressed on
toward nothing more than the figment of their fruitful imagi-
nations, an indomitable spirit, and an unslakable thirst for
endless new frontiers.

There were, of course, unfriendly Native Americans determined to kill the white intruders, but think, also, of the animals

that must have populated the nightmares of these new Americans from Europe. Mountain lions, alligators, wolverines, bison, panthers, grizzly bears, rattlesnakes. The rattlesnake—a deadly serpent not found anywhere else in the world—was a particularly frightening curiosity.

Wrote Benjamin Franklin about the American rattlesnake:

> I recollected that her eye excelled in brightness, that of any other animal, and that she has no eye-lids. She may therefore be esteemed an emblem of vigilance. She never begins an attack, nor, when once engaged, ever surrenders: She is therefore an emblem of magnanimity and true courage. As if anxious to prevent all pretensions of quarreling with her, the weapons with which nature has furnished her, she conceals in the roof of her mouth, so that, to those who are unacquainted with her, she appears to be a most defenseless animal; and even when those weapons are shown and extended for her defense, they appear weak and contemptible; but their wounds however small, are decisive and fatal. Conscious of this, she never wounds 'till she has generously given notice, even to her enemy, and cautioned him against the danger of treading on her.[11]

In time, of course, the rattlesnake became a potent emblem of American pride and fierce independence. On drums, shields, and flags, the serpent appeared above the motto: "Don't tread on me."

Yet as terrifying and unyielding as the natural world around them was to the first colonists, settlers, and pioneers in America, it was a double-edged sword. Nature could be harsh. The elements could be fatal. One simple mistake could cost your entire family their lives. Ignorance was never forgiven. Yet, these early Americans also knew that they could not survive without the nature around them. Yes, they had to compromise with that world, but they soon learned that if they worked hard and were smart about it, that same brutal nature would give back to them. In fact, it could give them great, great rewards. And they would realize that they could not survive without the bounty from that same nature.

In time, these early Americans discovered that you could do so much more than simply survive off nature. With industry and hard work, you could thrive. And with even more industry and hard work, you could begin to tame nature to the point that it worked for you. They knew instinctively that God had given them dominion over nature, but when two-thirds of your colony dies in the first winter in the New World, it can be hard to believe that you do indeed have dominion over nature. However, it was more than just a religious argument to these pious people. It was a political belief as well. For if the rights of man derived directly from God—the radical concept ultimately hatched by our Founders—then that means man is somehow special on Earth. Man is not just another animal. Man is made in God's image.

God specifically gave man the directive to be a good steward of nature—and to take control over it. We should not be unnecessarily cruel to animals or wantonly destroy nature. Rather we should use both judiciously to the benefit of ourselves and our families and our neighbors. Most Americans take that directive pretty seriously. The entire construct of Kosher food, for example, revolves around ensuring that the harvesting of animals has been done in a meticulously humane manner.

THE LEFTIST WAR ON HUMANS

Today, this history has been turned upside down. The militant Left places more importance on the rights of trees and animals over people. At the heart of this belief system is a revulsion for humanity on the part of the radical Left. Think this is an exaggeration? Some of the most prominent members of the environmental movements have said essentially the same thing.

Ingrid Newkirk, the founder of People for the Ethical Treatment of Animals (PETA), for instance, said that "Humans have grown like a cancer. We're the biggest blight on the face of the earth."[12]

According to Newkirk, humans do not have an inherent right to life. "I don't believe human beings have the 'right to life,'" she once said. "That's a supremacist perversion. A rat is a pig is a dog is a boy."[13]

Newkirk has gone so far as to issue a public will for her body to be donated to PETA upon her death with the direction that her body be used "in a manner that draws attention to needless animal suffering and exploitation."[14] While she leaves the particulars up to PETA, she recommends "that the 'meat' of my body, or a portion thereof, be used for a human barbecue, to remind the world that the meat of a corpse is all flesh, regardless of whether it comes from a human being or another animal and that flesh foods are not needed."[15]

Another recommendation is that her skin be peeled off and made into purses "to remind the world that human skin and the skin of other animals is the same and that neither is 'fabric.'" She suggests that her feet be removed and turned into an umbrella stand, you know, like the ones made out of elephant feet. No, thanks. She wants her liver "vacuum-packed and shipped" to France for foie gras. Anyway, you get the idea. The woman is nuts, but her movement and her cause are quite serious.

Philosopher John Hardwig argues that humanity is a drain on our natural resources and that humans get to a certain age where they have a "duty to die." He contends "there may be a fairly common responsibility to end one's life in the absence of any terminal illness . . . a duty to die when one would prefer to live. . . . To have reached the age of, say 75 or 80 years without being ready to die is itself a moral failing, the sign of a life out of touch with life's basic realities . . . A duty to die is more likely when you have already lived a rich and full life. You have already had a full share of the good things life offers."[16]

Some have even gone so far as to cheer terrible diseases like AIDS to cull the herd of humanity. "I know social scientists who remind me that people are part of nature, but it isn't true," claimed David Graber, a research biologist at the National Park Service (in other words, a government employee whose salary is paid by you, the taxpayer). "Somewhere along the line—at about a billion years ago and maybe half that—we quit the contract and became a cancer. We have become a plague upon ourselves and upon the earth. . . . Until such time as Homo sapiens should decide to rejoin nature, some of us can only hope for the right virus to come along."[17] If that's the way government employee Mr. Graber feels, then he can get a buffalo to pay his salary instead of Mr. and Mrs. America.

"AIDS is not a malediction, but the welcome and natural remedy to reduce the population of the planet," said the so-called environmentalist David Foreman, founder of a group called Earth First! "Should human beings disappear, I surely wouldn't mind."[18] I guess I wouldn't mind all that much if nutty David Foreman disappeared, but I'd rather the rest of humanity keep right on swinging. By the way, this Foreman guy also outlined his "goal" to reduce the global human population to about 100 million worldwide.[19] In other words, find some way to eliminate billions of people. Just a guess—this Grizzly Adams doesn't have a lot of friends.

Neither, I'd guess, does Paul Watson, an early member (and alleged founder) of the Left-wing environmental extremist group Greenpeace. "I reject the idea that humans are superior to other life forms. . . . Man is just an ape with an overly developed sense of superiority."[20] And environmentalist human hater Reed Noss noted, "The collective needs of non-human species must take precedence over the needs and desires of humans."[21]

"Animal rights have been top of mind for Americans in

recent years because of an increasing number of films and news stories depicting the poor treatment of animals," Gallup reports. "Congress requested a review of a government-funded animal research lab in late 2014, and cosmetics testing on animals was banned in the European Union in 2013."

As a result, Ringling Brothers have announced they will retire circus elephants by 2018. SeaWorld is phasing out their killer whale shows in San Diego. These decisions come after well-publicized accusations of cruelty to the elephants and killer whales in the shows. Also, this kind of entertainment has been deemed "disrespectful to animals," Gallup found. "Organized segments of the American public are very vocal about protecting animal rights, with groups such as People for the Ethical Treatment of Animals (PETA) even creating advertisements for prime-time events such as the Super Bowl.[22]"

Here's what I find so baffling about these people who claim to care so much about animals. I mean, how do they know that the animals don't like to be in the shows? Because elephants have sad eyes? Is that why they think it is cruel? Well, they have no idea what elephants like and don't like. It's like the horse-drawn carriages in Central Park. How does anybody know that those horses don't like drawing carriages? Have these people ever talked to the owners of these horses—owners who love their horses very much? Owners who have devoted their professional lives to keeping and maintaining these horses? Instead, some college kid with too much time on her hands and no job comes along and sees the horse, head down and looking sad-faced and then decides right there on the spot that the horse and its fellow horses are miserable and it is cruel to have them pulling carriages. Do they think the horses would be happier going off to the glue factory? Because, I am telling you, without this job, these horses don't have any other job. There isn't a huge job market out there for big, slow draft horses these days.

These people, though, have ginned this whole thing up into such a huge manufactured crisis that the mayor of New York

City spends weeks on end completely consumed by what to do about the freaking horses drawing carriages in Central Park. We are doomed.

PETA: SERIAL KILLERS

Of all the wacko and crazy Leftist scams PETA has pulled, few are more despicable and disgusting than the comic books and cartoons they use to target children in their campaign to allegedly prevent cruelty to animals, even at the cost of attacking the relationships between a mother and her children. In one of their most offensive campaigns, PETA activists handed out comic-art flyers to children accompanying women who wore fur outside holiday performances of *The Nutcracker*. The graphic pamphlet shows a woman with red lipstick, pearls, a yellow hair bun, and crazed, blue eyes gripping a terrified rabbit by the ears while stabbing it with a bowie knife. The bunny is pleading, but blood—the exact color of her lipstick—is spurting all over the place. She is wearing an apron. The words on top read: "Your mommy KILLS animals!"[23] On the bottom of the flyer, just above the pool of bunny blood, the comic instructs children: "Ask your mommy how many animals she killed to make her fur coat? The sooner she stops wearing fur, the sooner animals will be safe!"[24]

I am sorry, but you really have gone around the bend if you place such a high premium on animals that you would disturb the human relationship between mothers and their children. That is seriously messed up and might qualify as a certifiable illness. Like, maybe these people should be institutionalized. Even more amazing, though, is how hypocritical it is for PETA to attack mothers and their children for supposed cruelty to animals when, in fact, PETA itself has been exposed for killing, literally, tens of thousands of animals in its care.

Dating back to 1998, according to records provided by the Virginia Department of Agriculture and Consumer Services to

the Center for Consumer Freedom, the animal rights group kills
hundreds of household pets every year in facilities it ironically
calls "animal shelters." In 2014, PETA took in 2,631 animals in
Virginia. Thirty-nine were adopted. A shocking 2,324 were
killed. The rest were transferred to other facilities. Between
1998 and 2014, according to the records, PETA killed 33,514
household pets.[25] In one Norfolk, Virginia, branch of PETA,
documents disclosed the organization killed almost all of its
animals—that's according to a report in the reliably liberal *Huffington Post,* which was accompanied by a graphic entitled "For
An Animal Rights Organization, PETA Kills A Lot Of Animals." No kidding.[26]

PETA claimed that the reason for killing so many thousands
of animals in Virginia was because death is preferable to homelessness for them. It doesn't explain, however, how Maya the
Chihuahua wound up dead in 2014. Maya was a beloved member of Wilbur Cerate's family on Virginia's Eastern Shore.
One Saturday in October when Cerate came home from work,
according to local TV station WAVY, Maya was gone. Cerate
checked his security cameras, which had captured video of two
women in a PETA van backing into the driveway, snatching
Maya off the porch and driving off. Three days later, two women
from PETA returned to the home and explained that Maya had
been killed. They brought a fruit basket.[27, 28]

Perhaps it was the tiniest bit of solace for Cerate's little daughter
that her beloved Maya did not die a painful death, other than
the terror of being snatched up by strangers and hauled to some
foreign facility that, at best, must have seemed like a veterinarian's
office. Many of the other animals who die at the hands of bird-
brained animal-rights activists suffer horrible deaths.

In Idaho, July 2015, a pair of hipsters were charged under the
Animal Enterprise Terrorism Act for a forty-thousand-mile
cross-country crime spree that, well, ended badly. In addition
to vandalizing businesses and private homes and slashing tires
of people they suspected of animal cruelty, the couple "freed"

some 6,000 weasels from farms in five different states, according to TV station KTVB. They released 1,800 from a mink farm
in Burley, Idaho.[29] The farm manager was able to recapture most
of them, but, tragically, since minks are fed by machines, they
ran to the sound of engines on the nearest highway, looking to
be fed. "They're a domesticated animal out there," farm manager Mark Moyle explained. "Unfortunately, what they did
wasn't humane because now they're getting run over on the
highway."[30]

A group calling itself the Animal Liberation Front claimed
responsibility for the raid and a press officer named Jerry Vlasak
applauded the actions. "I have no idea if these two people that
have been arrested are the ones that did that," he said. "If they
did, they're our heroes. Whoever did it, they're our heroes."
Vlasak compared the crime spree to battles for civil rights
throughout history. "Any struggle for liberation, whether it was
against apartheid in South Africa, against slavery in this country, whether it was against any of the illegal occupations in other
countries like Vietnam or Iraq—all of these actions, all of these
liberation struggles have involved breaking the law to help those
who are being oppressed, and the struggle for animal liberation
is no different," he said.[31] Oh, my, what are these sad kids learning in school?

The Idaho mink operation, obviously, is nothing new. Crazed
activists have been freeing—and killing—minks for decades all
over the world. And, without exception, these "liberations" always end badly—no matter what your view of animal rights
may be. After a 2003 weasel release in a small town in Washington state, it wasn't just the mink farmers who were upset.
Months after the ten thousand minks were "freed," animals that
had not been rounded up or killed were still slaughtering
local ducks, chickens, exotic birds, family pets, and fingerling
salmon—not exactly animal-friendly behavior. And even the
ones that got rounded up didn't necessarily fare so well. Noto-
riously vicious, minks must be kept separated. Only littermates

can share cages. Unfortunately, though, since there was no telling which were siblings, all the weasels had to be rounded up and caged together, whereupon their natural instincts kicked in and they all started killing and eating one another.

At some level, I can understand the urge to "free" animals from a bad situation. I guess you might say my wife and I were involved in a small "liberation" effort ourselves once. It started when my show's former producer and our family's longtime friend, Sergio Gor, sat down for lunch with his friend Chris Wirth at a Chinese restaurant in New York. Sergio noticed some turtles swimming around in big tanks, and after some investigation, he discovered that the back rooms were full of not just turtles, but frogs, birds, baby goats, and all sorts of creatures. Apparently, you picked what you wanted to eat and they slaughtered it for you. Makes for a charming atmosphere, I'm sure.

Sergio knew something wasn't right, and the first person he called was my wife, Adrienne, who he knew to be a very serious animal lover with a particular soft spot for turtles. He told her what he'd found, and Adrienne jumped into action. "Buy the turtles," she told Sergio, "and we will save them." So, that's what Sergio and Chris did. They bought all the turtles in the restaurant and brought them back to the Fox News studios in a big box. That evening, I took the box home, and Adrienne and I took a look inside.

We'd been expecting the small, pet-sized turtles that fit in the palm of your hand. These were a lot bigger—basically miniature sea turtles—and here they were, just hanging out in our kitchen! Yet the important thing was that they were out of danger. We found a habitat for them, and they ended up with a good home. This "liberation" story is an example of looking out for animals by removing them from a bad spot. Sergio and Adrienne were in a position to save these turtles, and they did— but they did it smartly, without reckless action like the Idaho goofballs, which only ended up hurting the animals worse.

ANIMALS AS HUMANS

In the Leftists' war on humans, it is not enough just to denigrate humans and human needs as compared to animals. Part of their campaign is to also—literally—humanize animals. Dress them up. Give them rights. Make them go through all the rituals and routines humans do. And it all starts innocently enough.

We include our beloved pets in our Christmas cards as fully integrated members of our family. According to a 2011 Harris Poll, 91 percent of pet owners said they consider their pets to be members of their family,[32] which I totally get. I really do love animals. Dogs especially. The best dog in the world, of course, is the Bolling family's rescue mutt, Freedom. He's a mix of German shepherd and who the hell knows what else. We regularly send donations of dog food—literally truckloads from Iams, purchased and organized by Adrienne—to our local shelters to help out Freedom's buddies who just haven't found that special human to take them home yet. At some level, though, as much as we all love him, he is still a dog.

Yet if you walk around the city or go to dog parks anywhere in America, you might get the idea that some folks really are not sure that their pets are not actual human beings. They buy them only the most expensive dog food—that is, "human quality." Meaning we could eat it, and many of these people do. No, thanks! Then they dine with their pets at the table and dress them up in sweaters, booties, hats, raincoats, scarves. Anything you find at Macy's for humans, you can now find for dogs and cats. Down to the springy headbands and Happy New Year glasses that people put on their pets as they kiss them to ring in the new year. Like I said, I get it. But it's a little over the top, don't you think?

And then there was the "wedding" that took place in New York in January 2016. I am not making this up. The formal announcement went out thusly:

Toast and Finn's love story began when they met at a charity gala and instantly became best friends. With approval from Toast's dad, Finn popped the question on a beautiful fall day in Central Park and asked Toast to be his wife. Toast is greatly looking forward to walking down the aisle in her custom Marchesa gown.[33]

The thing is, she walked down the aisle on four legs. Toast and Finn are two small lapdogs. And they got married. At a high-end hotel in Manhattan. And, of course, both dogs have their own Instagram accounts. Naturally. Toast, the "bride," has 340,000 followers and Finn, the "groom," has 16,000 followers.[34]

"Arriving at the grand refectory of the High Line Hotel, I saw what looked a whole lot like a typical wedding: well-dressed guests in suits and gowns, clutching glasses of champagne and taking iPhone photos," reported one of the guests. "Just one difference from most weddings: The dull roar of human chatter and techno music was punctuated with the occasional bark or growl, and many of these well-dressed guests were clutching leashes, which were attached to dogs of every sort."[35]

GLOWING SUPERMARKETS

One of the biggest causes for the alarming disconnect in this country between animal rights insanity and the reality that our Founders understood is that, quite frankly, we have largely solved the single greatest physical threat that man has faced since the beginning of time: hunger. Now, I know there are people in America who still go to bed hungry at night. But they should not. Thanks to brilliant farming practices, efficient transportation, and the development of a relatively free and vibrant economy, America has created a nearly limitless bounty to feed not only us, but much of the rest of the world. Yet it comes at a cost. While our supermarket aisles are spilling over with fresh produce and glowing red meats and breads and just about anything you could possibly need, we have also lost connections to the places where it all comes from. Few of us know our own farmer. And if you do, you pay dearly for it! Yet there was a time when even if our parents or grandparents didn't know the farm where the steak came from, they did know the butcher. And that butcher knew the farmer who raised that cow or finished it and sold it at the meat market.

It used to be that among the first great moments in a boy's life was going hunting with his dad or his brother or his grandpa. First, the boy would just watch and hold his ears when birds flew over and guns started blasting every which way. The boy would eventually build up his courage and pick up and hold a dead bird. Death is very serious to a boy and he might stroke the soft, silky feathers of the dead bird. Then one day, the boy would be dispatched to retrieve a downed bird, only to find the bird just wounded and flopping around with a broken wing and scared eyes. The boy scoops up the bird and races back to his father and declares the bird must be saved. This conversation with his father is one of the most important moments in the boy's life. The father must take the bird and explain to the boy that it would be cruel to shoot and wound a bird, and then try to nurse it back to life. No, the purpose here is to hunt and kill this bird so they can eat it. The father will then wring the bird's neck so the boy understands just how gravely serious it is to hunt God's creatures.

For some boys, that was the last time they would go hunting. And that was usually totally fine. Some people have that extra gene of compassion that makes them unable to kill any animal under any circumstances, but they are better for having faced the blood and the lead and the feathers. At least they understand where it all comes from. And for most boys—and girls!—the experience is a little traumatizing at first. But then they grow from it and gain wisdom from it and become more thoughtful from it and they spend the rest of their lives responsibly harvesting God's creatures to feed their families, and these people are the greatest conservationists of nature in our society.

Last winter, hunter Jerry Kinnaman was bow hunting in southeast Missouri when a monstrous 10-point buck walked into view at about eighty-five yards, easily within range for the experienced hunter. He drew his bow and released the arrow, killing the beast. Even before he reached the dead animal, Kinnaman knew he had just kicked a hornets nest. The seven-and-a-half-year-old deer was a rare ghost-white albino and had become something of a celebrity around Cape Girardeau. And, sure enough, it was only a matter of time before the death threats started rolling in. "People are all tough on the computer," he told the local newspaper. "But it's easy for them to say that because they know they're not going to get in trouble for it."[36]

Now I get why people might get upset over killing a local celebrity rare albino deer. What was interesting was that Kinnaman understood it as well. In fact, he said, he had passed up shooting the deer for years. He watched him grow into a full-grown beast. And, finally, deep into the buck's life, Kinnaman began to realize that the animal was losing weight and had become sickly and, he figured, he would not make it through the winter. So, instead of letting the animal die and vanish beside some creek, Kinnaman harvested the albino deer. "I gave him a fair shot. He had a good life," Kinnaman told the *Southeast Missourian* newspaper. "He's famous. He still will be."[37]

Just as important as feeding ourselves and our families, the proper use of animals has done miraculous things in man's never-ending quest to find cures for diseases and pinpoint things in the world that are bad for humans. Rarely have animals provided more for humans than during the summer of 1921, when researchers Frederick Banting and Charles Best identified and were learning to manufacture a new miracle cure called insulin. If it could be proved effective and safe, they believed it could be used to give people suffering the horrific, wasting disease of

diabetes a full and normal life. Yet before the thousands await-
ing the ultimate diabetes death sentence could be helped, this
new insulin had to be proven. And it was dogs—dozens after
dozens of them—that Banting and Best had at their disposal.
First, they had to make the dogs diabetic by removing their
pancreases. Then they had to keep them alive with shots of insulin. Agonizingly, the researchers lost many, many dogs that
summer in the sweltering lab, according to *Breakthrough: Elizabeth Hughes, the Discovery of Insulin, and the Making of a Medical
Miracle,* by Arthur Ainsberg and Thea Cooper. Finally, Dog 92,
a collie, did the unthinkable: On August 31, 1921, the dog
died—an astonishing twenty days after Banting and Best had
removed her pancreas. She had been kept alive—and for much
of the time quite healthy—on injected insulin. "I shall never
forget that dog as long as I shall live," Banting later wrote. "I
have seen patients die and I have never shed a tear. But when
that dog died I wanted to be alone for the tears would fall despite
anything I could do."[38] In a matter of months, thanks to Dog
92, insulin was being approved and manufactured for human
use. It is estimated that the breakthrough provided by that dog
has saved the lives of more than 16 million humans and extended
the lives of hundreds of millions more.

CARING FOR ANIMALS AND NATURE

The dirty secret about these animal-rights wackos is that animals really have no greater enemy. They do not understand the
animals they claim to care so much about. They have no idea
how those animals think and what makes them happy. It's like
when they go set ten thousand weasels free and the weasels all
head for the nearest highway. Or wipe out a local exotic bird
population. Or attack family pets. Or eat one another.

In truth, the greatest friends these animals have are the people
who care for them: farmers who learn how their cattle and horses
and pigs think. And in the case of wildlife, nobody cares more

about animals than hunters. Duck hunters love ducks and spend millions of dollars every year establishing habitats for them and ensuring that they survive and thrive. Deer hunters develop habitats for deer all year long and provide crucial, humane harvesting that wildlife biologists say cuts down on diseases among deer, culls weak or sick from herds, and reduces the number of harrowing deer versus car accidents that horribly maim deer and often injure humans.

This goes for nature as well. Take trees, for example. Nobody in America plants more trees every year than the forestry industry. According to a report by the U.S. Forest Service, the forest industry plants 45 percent of all new trees planted each year. Another 42 percent are planted by private landowners who plant, grow, harvest, and sell their matured trees to the forest industry. The federal government plants just about 6 percent.[39] In other words, if it were not for the forest industry and the commercial demand for wood and other tree products, the United States would lose 87 percent of new trees planted each year. The known benefits of trees are endless. They scrub and store carbon dioxide, they produce oxygen, scrub pollution from the air, cool temperature—particularly in cities—and provide endless habitats for animals. Also, they are nice to look at.

If you like trees, you should thank the forestry industry because without that industry, America would have far, far, far fewer trees. Which is one major reason why we have so much more forestland in America today than we did eighty or a hundred years ago. "Forest growth nationally has exceeded harvest since the 1940s," according to a report by the Food and Agriculture Organization. "By 1997, forest growth exceeded harvest by 42 percent and the volume of forest growth was 380 percent greater than it had been in 1920."[40]

You will never hear any of this from humanity hater Ingrid Newkirk, PETA crazies, or their ignoramus acolytes on college campuses across the country. The indisputable truth, though, is that industry is and always has been nature's greatest friend in

America. It has been through the relatively free and vibrant economy that we can afford to set environmental standards and enforce sensible laws to stop wanton pollution of our air or waterways. If you have any doubt about this, visit a Third World country where indoor plumbing is as foreign as a flying car. And you know where people in those places go to wash? Right in the polluted river.

7. MERIT

noun mer·it \\'mer-ət, 'me-rət\

(1.) the quality of being good, important, or useful: value or worth
                                    —Merriam-Webster's definition

(1.) a false, bigoted, and usually racist notion that some people are better at certain tasks than others; praising the few ahead of the needs of the collective
                                    —A Leftist's definition

It seems to never occur to fools that merit and good fortune are closely united.

— JOHANN WOLFGANG VON GOETHE

In October 2009, Barack Obama was awarded the Nobel Peace Prize. This used to be considered the highest honor conferred on any human being—only two other sitting Presidents had won it. Theodore Roosevelt received it for negotiating an end to the Russo-Japanese War that threatened the stability of Asia, and even the world. Woodrow Wilson was awarded the prize for his role in developing the League of Nations.[1]

What had Barack Obama done? What great dispute had he solved? What was his titanic contribution to world peace that required him receiving this high honor after less than nine months in office?[2]

Let's do a quick review:

- He was born and made it through elementary school, middle school, and high school.

- Attended several elite educational institutions, including Occidental College, Columbia University, and Harvard Law School.[3]
- Worked as something called "a community organizer."[4]
- Served in the Illinois State Senate.[5]
- Gave a really good speech at the 2004 Democratic National Convention.[6]
- Served in the United States Senate.[7]
- Gave a lot of speeches and picked a lot of smart political operatives to help him run for President of the United States.
- Got elected President.

I wasn't the only one asking: Am I missing something here?

According to the Nobel Committee (the group of ultra-liberals in Norway who pick the prize winners), Obama was awarded the 2009 prize "for his extraordinary efforts to strengthen international diplomacy and cooperation between peoples."[8] Really? After less than a year in office? This was an award modeled after *Seinfeld*—it truly was about nothing, and meant nothing, at least in reality.

Even the Obama administration had the good grace to be embarrassed by the award. Besides giving an abysmally naïve "speech to the Muslim world" in Cairo and talking about things like nuclear nonproliferation and climate change, the man had done squat in terms of forwarding world peace in the months he had been in office. He said so himself: "To be honest, I do not feel that I deserve to be in the company of so many of the transformative figures who've been honored by this prize."[9] Though the administration was not quite embarrassed enough to show the good grace of declining the honor in favor of someone who actually deserved it.

But here's why this award matters—because it fits so perfectly with Leftist philosophy. Obama was a global rock star who had replaced the "evil" George W. Bush. He was also the first African American to lead the United States. And the Nobel Committee wanted to do what felt good. They wanted in on the action. Essentially, this once-prestigious organization decided to act like squealing teenagers at a Beatles concert; they got caught up in "Obamamania" and just couldn't help themselves. It felt good, so it felt right. So they did it.

And then this Nobel Laureate went on to spend eight years undermining world peace by kneecapping the one thing that keeps a lid on this bubbling cauldron of a world: the U.S. military. He also invaded and destabilized Libya, broke his promises on Syria, has been downright dismissive to Israel, kowtowed to China, and let Russian President Vladimir Putin walk all over him (and therefore us). This man has done more to destabilize the world than perhaps any American President, ever. And guess what? Even the Nobel Committee who scrambled to award him the prize came to regret their decision! The Nobel Institute's director at the time told the media in September 2015 that they "thought it would strengthen Obama and it didn't have this effect," and "even many of Obama's supporters thought that the prize was a mistake."[10] Oops.

The idea of "merit"—so fundamental to the American system of government and culture—is based on a simple formula: People should succeed based on their own skills, talents, and efforts, not because it makes somebody "feel good" or because of some arbitrary societal or governmental standard.

Today, achieving something based on your own drive, skill, or merit is anathema to liberals in politics, media, and academia. For all their talk about "income inequality," a "living wage," and "fairness," liberals really just think they and their cronies know better than the rest of us. They want us to believe that America can and should be run by liberal elites—technocrats who have more education than sense, and a more-than-robust sense of entitlement. And what do these elites do? Maintain the status quo so they can stay in power and continue to control the levers of our society.

In short, among the many principles considered vices by the

Left is exceptionalism, both for individuals and for the United States as a nation. Nobody is better than anyone else; we're all just products of our environment, and should be treated accordingly. They think we are born blank slates upon which to stamp one identity or another. They think the United States is just one nation among many, as capable of good or evil as any other country. They don't believe we have a special role to play in human events; that God created the United States to point the way—to be a "shining city upon a hill" as Ronald Reagan so eloquently cribbed John Winthrop[11]—to show the world how a country and society can and should be based on freedom, equality, and opportunity.

But here's the thing: People and nations do have different, inherent talents, skills, abilities—strengths and weaknesses—and should be allowed to rise or fall based on them. Not everyone can be a rock star, pro athlete, or business tycoon. There's nothing wrong with people who aren't exceptional, but to act as if they are the same as those who are exceptional does a major disservice to both. Failing to praise the God-given talents of exceptional Suzy stifles her ambitions; undeservedly praising the "talents" of unexceptional Jane hurts Suzy by not recognizing her talents (and efforts), while setting Plain Jane up for failure and disappointment.

Unlike today's junior soccer games, in the game of life, not everyone gets a trophy. Some people do. Some people's trophies are bigger than others', some get trophies they don't want. Some get nothing at all. That's just how it is. But remember, liberals are "magical thinkers." They don't live in reality. They see the trophy and the turd and really believe they are essentially the same thing—it's just that the person holding the turd must have been held back by a lack of opportunity, racism, sexism, or whatever "-ism" is in vogue (have you ever wondered what a better world we'd live in if liberals had more "-asms" and fewer "-isms" in their lives?). Whatever it is, it is always something out of their control, so they can't be held accountable. And the government will be right there to make sure everything turns out to be "fair."

What liberals and their cult of "fairness" don't seem to realize is how unfair this attitude is to those who *are* exceptional (and how destructive it is to a vibrant society). Imagine Mozart as a child attending a precious, liberal preschool today. While his teachers would almost certainly recognize his talent, they would as often as not try to squelch it, at least when other kids are around, lest they trouble the fragile self-image of his classmates. Had liberals been in charge, Mozart might never have created some of the greatest pieces of music in human history.

How many little Mozarts are out there right now being stifled by our "everyone gets a trophy" culture?

HEAD OF THE CLASS

I'm the son of two working-class parents. I was brought up on the northwest side of Chicago, in a tiny house on the fringes of a pretty well-off neighborhood. Yet I knew we didn't belong. For as long as I can remember, I knew we were poor. We were dead broke. As grown-ups, we might not realize it, but class differences are apparent to kids early on—we can pretend they aren't, but they are, and we should be honest with our kids about them. I learned where my family stood early on, because I had plenty to compare us to when I was growing up.

We lived on the outskirts of the relatively wealthy neighborhood of Sauganash. To be clear, we were technically in it, but not of it. My grandfather, my mother's father, had enjoyed a few years of limited prosperity and built four little houses huddled together on the edge of this affluent enclave, and of that he was justifiably proud. Unfortunately, his success was short-lived—but those are the breaks. As small as our house was, we never would have been able to afford even that if Grandpa hadn't given it to my mom—before he went bankrupt himself.

The rich folks in Sauganash didn't want much to do with us. They preferred to pretend our little cluster of homes didn't exist. Certainly nothing about us was fancy. Our car was a 1967 Buick Skylark that we drove into the ground—I once took a girl out on a date in that car only to have the whole back of the front bench seat fall backward when I put my foot on the brake (miraculously, she still opted to go out with me!).

My parents worked hard to make a good life for us, and as a very young kid, I didn't really notice our poverty. Then, when I hit middle school age, my mother got a second job so that my parents could afford to send me to Catholic school. This was the same school the rich Sauganash kids went to, and I was in for a rude awakening. I knew right away that my clothes weren't as nice as theirs, and that my house wasn't as big and fancy.

My family couldn't even afford to get me the same shoes all the other kids had seemed to have—PRO-Keds. They were just too expensive. I vividly remember the pain in my mother's eyes—and her embarrassment—when she told me we couldn't afford them, right there in the ValueVille discount store where she bought our shoes. I knew how hard my mom and dad worked. Despite all they did, they just couldn't afford those PRO-Keds. So I didn't get them, and I'm not going to deny that really, really sucked at the time. In the end, though, I'm glad that I never got them: I've been fighting for them ever since, and it's helped me get where I am today.

To some people, not being able to afford a pair of shoes probably doesn't seem like an earth-shattering loss, but if you grew up poor or working class like I did, these kinds of things stick with you. They define how you perceive yourself, and what "faction" of society you perceive as "yours." We all have inner perceptions of ourselves (well, except sociopaths and certain politicians). To poor and working-class kids like me, who grow up to immigrate to another "part" of society, we are still driven by memories of hardship, perseverance, and parental fortitude. It often defines our character, if not our current reality.

Anyway, instead of feeling sorry for myself because I couldn't have the shoes I wanted, I learned a very important lesson that day in the shoe store: I loved and respected my parents deeply, and always have. At the same time, I knew right then that I didn't want to grow up and bust my ass and still barely be able to put food on the table—let alone a pair of sweet PRO-Keds on my kid's feet.

I wanted to break out. Get rich. Succeed, like the people I saw on TV. I wasn't ashamed—and still am not—to say I want to make money. Lots and lots of money. Only those who have inherited wealth have the luxury of feeling ashamed of it. To those of us who know what it's like to not have enough, there is no shame in it at all. Money is freedom. It's having more control over your own life. In its rawest, purest state, it's simply one thing: power.

Achieving success—attaining this kind of power to control one's own destiny—is what we used to call the American Dream. And I wanted my piece of it . . . badly. Yet I didn't think anybody—including the government and society—owed me a damn thing. All I wanted was the chance to make something of myself. That's what first attracted me to sports. I may not have had the big house, nice car, or new clothes that the rich Sauganash kids had, but if I was going to go to school with them, I had to carve out my niche somehow, right?

I found it in athletics. Money can't buy talent, in sports or anything else. Talent only succeeds when matched with an iron will—pain, sweat, and deprivation in the pursuit of a singular goal. In sports, especially with baseball, I discovered that if I put in the work, I could be the equal of—and better than—anyone, no matter where they came from or how much money they had. If you play the game fairly, sports are the ultimate form of (and lesson in) meritocracy.

In sports, my hard work paid off and with results came respect, not just from my classmates, but my parents, too. They used to come to every game they could, which was tough since they both worked—Mom in town every day, and Dad on the road most of the time. But if they couldn't make a game, they'd just come watch a practice. Seeing their pride always inspired me to push myself—to always strive to do better. They inspire me to this day.

I'm willing to bet that some version of this story has been told millions of times since the first days of America. Trying to get ahead—to be exceptional, to seek merit—is nothing to be ashamed of (and if you think about how this country was founded and built, it's pretty horrifying that this even has to be stated). Achievement deserves rewards, but you have to actually work for your trophy. Just because liberals can't recognize this simple fact doesn't make it any less true.

The dedication and sacrifice of people like my parents are what made this country great, and helped countless families climb the economic ladder, even producing self-made billionaires like Bill Gates and Carl Icahn, who have created enormous amounts of wealth for our economy, and for a lot of other people, too.

HELICOPTER NATION

We've all heard of helicopter parents, but folks, let's face it: We live in a helicopter nation. Instead of our parents hovering over us watching our every move, it's the government, media, and PC watchdogs snooping into our lives, telling us how to think, talk, and act, and creating a kind of mind tyranny that is in absolute opposition to the Founders' vision.

Consider Thomas Jefferson's most famous line from the Declaration of Independence, and how abysmally wrong the Left is in its interpretation of it:

> We hold these truths to be self-evident, that all men are
> created equal, that they are endowed by their Creator
> with certain unalienable Rights, that among these are
> Life, Liberty and the pursuit of Happiness.

The key point here is that all people are *created* equal—not that all people *are* equal. Note the word "created." A higher power is at work in Jefferson's mind, and under this Creator's benevolent gaze, all human beings are of equal *value*—not equal character, strengths, and weaknesses. As children of the Creator, all should have the right to "Life, Liberty and the pursuit of Happiness," but we live our lives, exercise our liberty, and pursue our happiness according to our own strengths and weaknesses, talents and foibles, and good and bad tendencies.

In fact—and quite deliberately—what Jefferson says is that all people are not equal in character, ability, or work ethic, and therefore the ideal system of government keeps the proverbial playing field as level as possible so that each person can live life, enjoy liberty, and experience happiness unencumbered by an oppressive government.

However, that's not how the Left sees things—which is why we have nonsensical policies in place, despite the Founders' wisdom. For example, women in combat. In a vacuum, I have no problem with it. In fact, I think the military should have a single physical strength and endurance test and anyone who fails it—regardless of gender—should not be allowed to see combat. That's the very definition of fairness. That the majority of those who make it to the battlefield would be men is the result of a biological truth: On average, men are physically bigger and stronger than women. Some women would make it, too.

The reality, though, is unimportant to liberals, even if denying it means that our brave military members are put at risk. Instead of keeping the bar high and saying, "Hey, if you can reach it, you can fight," liberals want to lower the bar so that more women can go into combat—even if they cannot handle the physical rigors of doing so. This statement is not a slight on women. Women go through labor, so I am in no way doubting the fairer sex's mental and physical toughness. It's simply a question of strength, speed, and endurance.

Affirmative action is another example. There is no question

that from our nation's founding into the 1960s and 1970s institutional racism was endemic, and it was nearly impossible for black Americans to "make it" in the same way white Americans could. Affirmative action helped correct this horrible situation, and we now live in a country with true equality under the law, as well as widespread abhorrence of racism. Affirmative action worked. It's simply not necessary anymore.

Yet these amazing results weren't good enough for liberals. Today, they want to keep in place this same quota system well past its necessity. They push forward affirmative action that puts people in higher-educational institutions or the workforce based on quotas, instead of achievement and excellence. This perception—that minorities get placement in colleges or jobs because of their race or gender and not their abilities—is deeply harmful to the very people the Left claims it is helping. It's what George W. Bush once called "the soft bigotry of low expectations."

At the end of the day, the Left would love our nation to surrender to the false ideas that as a person:

- You are not special.
- You are not better than anyone else, at anything.
- You do not have to earn recognition.
- Everyone should receive equal treatment, equal benefits, and equal pay, regardless of their talents and work ethic— or the results they produce.

Regardless of the nature of a problem, the liberal solution is always that things would be better if everyone were just "treated the same." This systematic destruction of our nation's meritorious ethos—where people rise or fall based on their own talents and character—is in the end a destruction of the American way of life itself, and a corrosion of the American soul. When we pretend that everyone is the same—that everyone "deserves" the same rewards—we discourage the idea that a single person can achieve things that no one else can: crafting a piece of music, building a skyscraper, finding a cure for cancer.

This is truly helicopter parenting writ large. Welcome to America, my friends: helicopter nation. To the liberal mind, people cannot and should not be considered and treated as exceptional, or judged on their merit. The same goes for nations. When something bad happens, the knee-jerk liberal reaction is to assume that—somehow, somewhere—the United States is part of the problem.

I find this infuriating. Throughout our history—even after we became the "default" major power, like England, France, and Spain before us—we have approached the world with intentions as good as possible in a nation-state, especially one of our size and diversity. We are the most powerful nation that has ever existed, and yet we've tried to use this power to (mostly) do good. No other global power can claim the same; and we certainly should not be ashamed of our country.

That the United States is unexceptional—America itself no better than any other nation—is why liberals like President Obama can treat Iran and Cuba as if they are rational actors, despite having done nothing to earn this distinction. This is more of the liberals' magical thinking: If we just treat them like responsible members of the global community, they will be so overwhelmed by our wonderful system that they will eventually, spontaneously embrace sectarian tolerance and Jeffersonian democracy.

This thinking is why President Obama won the Nobel Peace Prize: not because he deserved it, but because it felt good and (importantly) his politics were right (read: liberal) and therefore deserved praise.

MERITOCRACY OR MEDIOCRITY?

We know all too well the societal consequences of the liberal approach to merit and exceptionalism: People are discouraged from standing out or believing in their specialness. If merit isn't valued, why work so hard to attain it? Such defeatist crap hasn't fully taken over our country—yet. Yet incredibly, a huge number of Americans think trying to make everyone equal is The Right Thing to Do.

Consider this: In a 2014 Reason-Rupe survey, 40 percent of Americans said, "all kids on a sport team should receive a trophy for their participation." Meanwhile, "57 percent of Americans think only the winning players" should receive trophies.[12]

Now let's break it down by political ideology: "Fully 66 percent of Republicans want only the kids who win to receive trophies, while 31 percent say all kids on the team should receive them." Democrats, meanwhile, "are evenly divided with 48 percent who say all kids, and another 48 percent who say only the winners should receive a trophy."[13]

There are three shocking results in this poll. The first is that 40 percent of our fellow Americans effectively think that people should be given the same rewards for unequal abilities and efforts. The second is that only half of Democrats feel this way (perhaps all is not lost?). The third is that one-third of Republicans feel the same—who are these Republicans and how can they be this clueless?

Another major consequence of the liberal approach to merit and achievement is that as a nation, we bail everyone out—from banks to homeowners to shopaholics—whether they deserve it or not. The bailouts after the 2008 market and housing crashes are a perfect example. The Wall Street bankers and their cronies in Washington got off scot-free despite almost bringing down the world economy. And millions of shortsighted or just plain stupid homeowners who bought houses they couldn't afford were bailed out as well.

And who paid for all this "bailing?" You and I—honest, responsible taxpayers. Basically, whether as a homeowner or investor (or both), if you were smart and prudent with your money, you got punished for it by having to pay for the mistakes of others. And those others? Well, us "bailers" must look like real suckers to them.

Many people forget that it was one of these mortgage bail-outs that helped set off the Tea Party movement in February 2009, when CNBC analyst Rick Santelli[14] went on a glorious rant on live TV about the unfairness of the responsible having to pay for the irresponsible, stating the "government is promoting bad behavior" and we're "thinking of having a Chicago Tea Party in July. All you capitalists that want to show up to Lake Michigan, I'm going to start organizing. . . . We're going to be dumping in some derivative securities."[15]

Here's the real meat of what Santelli said then, and what I'm saying now in a broader context:

> Why don't you put up a web site to have people vote on the Internet as a referendum to see if we really want to subsidize the losers' mortgages, or would we like to, at least, buy cars and buy houses in foreclosure and give them to people who might have a chance to actually prosper down the road, and reward people that could carry the water, instead of drink(ing) the water . . .

> This is America! How many of you people want to pay for your neighbors' mortgage that has an extra bathroom and can't pay their bills? . . . Y'know, Cuba used to have mansions and a relatively decent economy. They moved from the individual to the collective. Now they're driving '54 Chevys, maybe the last great car to come out of Detroit.[16]

That's when things began to change—when enough people got pissed off enough to fight back against the failed liberal system of government: The Tea Party was born, and has been fighting for commonsense, pro-America, pro-growth, and pro-individual liberty policies ever since. Yet there is still an enormous amount of work to be done.

In the past, the United States was a true market economy where one's merit directly impacted the outcomes of one's life. If you worked hard, followed the rules, and were willing to take some risks to get ahead, you would. That's how the market works. On the other side is a command economy, where the government is in charge of nearly every aspect of economic life (think the old USSR). Today, we're a "mixed" economy—but what about tomorrow? The United States is in the midst of a tectonic shift from a market economy to a command economy, and we've got to stop it before it goes any further.

Is the American meritocracy doomed? In a word: maybe. The sad fact is, one's merit (the algorithm of strengths, weaknesses, character, and work ethic we each possess) is not properly connected to outcomes and consequences in our society. With control of the media, academia, and a huge chunk of the political world, liberals have spent generations slowly moving average Americans from hardworking go-getters who are honored and respected because of their good attributes, to wimpy pools of insecurity always looking for things they don't deserve—a handout (and most certainly not a hand up). The radical Left's work isn't complete, but they have come a long way.

TRUMPED: THE DONALD EXAMPLE

The question of merit and exceptionalism is one of the many reasons it was so much fun watching elites of both parties stutter and stumble over the wild popularity among Republicans and many Independents of Donald Trump as a presidential candidate. What these elites fail to understand—what they always fail to understand—is that at core Americans don't want to be taken care of, they don't want to be "equal," and they don't want to get things that they don't deserve.

What they do want, though, is a fair shot of becoming exceptional themselves. Trump is an avatar of American exceptionalism at its best. Most Americans don't want to tax the Donald Trumps of the country into oblivion—they want to *be* the next Donald Trump. And they really, really don't want to pay for their neighbors' poor choices.

This is why the Donald's "no apologies" approach to attaining vast wealth and holding people accountable is so exciting to huge numbers of people. They like Trump because he speaks directly to these disillusioned, disaffected people (the "bailers"), and because they like the idea of him—that with enough toughness, hard work, and merit, they could be billionaires, too.

Donald Trump may not be some people's idea of an ideal President, but his confidence (in himself, and in America) and lack of artifice are a breath of fresh, meritorious air to Americans sick of being patted on the head and told to just let the elites handle things, keep working, and be prepared to bail out others when needed.

Look, there will always be lazy, stupid people in any society—those who don't value merit, or themselves. Historically, the United States has had these folks at lower rates than other countries. By nature, we are risk-takers, go-getters, and hardworking SOBs. More and more of us, though, are being convinced by the radical Left and their nanny-state, collectivist programs and philosophy that merit seeking is dangerous. If we don't treat everyone exactly the same, we're being "unfair." Better to just sit back and take what the government gives you and try to enjoy life as much as possible, right?

Wrong. Again, just look at the Tea Party movement—this is America at its finest. People spontaneously rebelling against the elites and their stifling, unfair agenda, as well as their lack of respect for regular, hardworking, responsible Americans and their dreams of bigger and better things. It's been a slog, but the Tea Party movement has made a positive difference for this nation. It's up to us to keep the struggle going for the soul of America.

"MAKING AMERICA GREAT AGAIN"
(As The Donald Says)

As Margaret Thatcher once said about her rise to prime minister, "I wasn't lucky, I deserved it."

On my own path to success, I often wasn't the smartest person in the room, or the handsomest, or the most charming. But I had my own assets. I had hustle, drive, and the determination to outwork every other SOB who crossed my path. That's what the American dream is all about—that people of good character and a willingness to work hard can leverage their natural abilities (and overcome their weaknesses) to create an exceptional life for themselves.

While class and access to resources always have (and always will) give some people a head start, anybody—and I mean *anybody*—can make something of themselves in this country if they are willing to take risks, work hard, and be responsible for their own actions. Yeah, sometimes you'll lose your shirt. But you get up, dust yourself off, try again—and you go get another damn shirt.

As we've seen with the Tea Party movement and strong support for presidential candidates like Donald Trump, more and more Americans are waking up to the reality that the country they live in isn't the country they were born in. And we're starting to fight back and gain ground. The growth of talk radio and other conservative news outlets, along with impactful websites and blogs that engage directly to the grassroots have transformed the media landscape so that conservative voices can now get through to at least some people.

Try as they may, the liberal media gatekeepers who have been complicit in brainwashing our citizens can no longer hold back the tide of sanity being driven by exactly the kind of hardworking, tough-as-nails regular folks who used to be the majority of this country.

As a nation, it's time for us to choose. Will we continue down the path we're already on, which, in the Left's grand plan, ends in a European-style society where everyone is forced to be mediocre and average, and merit is discouraged or even punished? Or will we remain American, encouraging folks to work hard to become an outlier (i.e., exceptional)? I know what I'd choose—and what all those Tea Party and Trump supporters would choose as well.

Tyranny rarely comes riding in at the head of an army—it usually creeps into a society in small ways that over time becomes Orwellian shackles. However, if the sane and smart among us stand up, speak out, vote for real change, and stop being afraid of stepping on people's toes, we can take our country back.

8. PRIDE

noun \'prīd

(1.) a feeling that you respect yourself and deserve to be respected by other people
—Merriam-Webster's definition

(1.) a shameful feeling that wrongly places the individual above the collective

(2.) a wrongheaded belief that any nation or group is somehow more special than any other
—A Leftist's definition

"National honor is national property of the highest value."
—JAMES MONROE

I'm named Eric Bolling because of an uncle I never knew. Uncle Eric was shot down by the Japanese over the islands then called the New Hebrides in the South Pacific. Now they're known as the nation of Vanuatu, and Japan is an ally and trading partner rather than a totalitarian aggressor, because of the sacrifices of men like my Uncle Eric, who gave his life in defense of America, a nation he loved.

Is there anyone in the world today, if given a choice, who wouldn't be an American citizen? I doubt there are many. Which is why millions every year make their way here, legally and illegally, because they know this is the greatest country on earth.

Why is it, then, that so many people outside America believe that—and yet so many actual Americans don't?

America, we have a pride problem. Do we know what we stand for? Do we know what America is? Is it okay to be patriotic in polite company anymore? The sad truth is our appreciation of the unique set of values that motivated our Founders and set America apart in the world is on the wane. The young people of America are uninformed and largely unimpressed with their own country. Because they didn't live through two world wars and the Cold War, because they are totally ignorant of Soviet gulags and China's mass murder of its citizens and never heard of Pol Pot, they don't see America as any different from any nation on earth. They are susceptible to the rants of coddled celebrities—whose multiple plastic surgeries and dye jobs have warped their brains—preaching about how ashamed they are to live in this country. In the last year or so, another of these entitled, foolish singers—this one named Ariana Grande—was caught on video in a shop licking unpurchased donuts and saying, "I hate Americans. I hate America."[1]

And, lest we forget, even First Lady Michelle Obama got into this pathetic, embarrassing act when she proclaimed she wasn't proud of America throughout her entire adult life, until her husband was elected President.[2] Really, Mrs. Obama? Really?

Frankly, I don't care what these rich grievance collectors have to say. Hating America is the trendy thing to spout on about in their elitist circles. Of course, I notice most of these people still live in America and still take advantage of Americans who buy their songs or go to their films or vote for their husbands.

What I worry about is those who don't know any better. Those who don't remember that many of our ancestors left their home countries with nothing more than the clothes on their back, a willingness to work, and the abiding knowledge that opportunity abounded in a nation founded as a beacon of liberty, commerce, and religious freedom. They toiled in factories and lived crammed in tenement apartments, with the understanding that this country would reward their hard work in a way that no other could. They took great pride in the knowledge that their children would have a better life, and an even greater set of opportunities. They fought two world wars against totalitarian governments that stood as the antithesis to those American ideals, and then lived under the shadow of a Cold War. During that time, the children, grandchildren, and great-grandchildren of those Eastern European, Irish, and Italian immigrants that passed through Ellis Island moved from the tenements to the trades to the top of America's legal and financial professional world. As the infamous boxing promoter Don King was fond of saying, "Only in America."

It's sad to say, but today, those same lower Manhattan streets are more likely to be littered with those hardworking Americans' entitled descendants: spoiled Millennials and their tenured liberal academic mentors. Demanding freedom from responsibility, free college, free health care, and a high salaried job in the career of their choice, with none of the sweat and hard work the rest of us put in, the Americans of today don't want opportunity, they want handouts.

What happened? We lost our sense of national pride, and with it our understanding of what makes America a great nation.

In the aftermath of the tragic September 11 attacks, a Gallup poll found that 70 percent of Americans were extremely proud of their country. We had just faced a very hostile attack on our values from an enemy that hated everything we were, and we came together like never before with a renewed sense of national pride. By 2015, that number had gone down to 54 percent, with an eye-popping 19 percent of Americans expressing that they're either moderately, a little, or not proud at all. Unsurprisingly, Democrats and Millennials are the culprits here. Only 47 percent of Democrats were extremely proud of their country, with only 43 percent of Millennials expressing extreme pride.[3]

Sure, some of these folks probably do have something against their own country. They're lost causes, and can pack up and leave for their socialist paradises as far as I'm concerned. For a lot of Americans, though, who don't express pride in their country, the real problem might be ignorance. Shockingly and shamefully, too few understand what sets America apart. We have no idea what we're supposed to be proud of.

Our school system and politicians seem to have failed at inspiring this pride in us. An Annenberg Public Policy Center poll conducted in 2014 found that 36 percent, or more than one-third (!) of Americans couldn't name the three branches of government.[4] In 2011, *Newsweek* took a random sample of a thousand Americans and asked them a set of basic civics questions. The results were depressing. Seventy-three percent of respondents couldn't explain why we fought the Cold War. Forty-four percent of Americans could not explain the Bill of Rights, and 6 percent couldn't say when Independence Day fell in the year.[5]

It's even worse when you ask people about the concepts that define America. A 2015 Newseum poll found that 57 percent of the 1,002 people surveyed didn't know that the First Amendment includes the right to free speech. Only 10 percent named freedom of the press and freedom of assembly, and 19 percent named freedom of religion.[6] Another poll, conducted by the Intercollegiate Studies Institute, found that more people could identify *American Idol* judge Paula Abdul than could identify the phrase "government of the people, for the people, and by the people" with Abraham Lincoln's famous Gettysburg Address.[7]

If that's not bad enough, young Americans are as entitled as they are ignorant of their history. A recent Rupe-Reason poll found that two-thirds of Americans think the term "entitled" describes eighteen- to twenty-nine-year-old Americans very well or quite well.[8] Another unfortunate poll bears out what this means in real terms. *The Washington Times* reported that an overwhelming 60 percent of Millennials support sending in ground troops to combat ISIS, but 62 percent would not want to join the fight themselves, *even if* the United States needed additional troops.[9] Radical Islam is the latest in a long line of terribles—monarchy, communism, and fascism—faced down by American patriots. Call me crazy, but I have a hard time believing the young men who fought those earlier battles would be quite as unenthusiastic about serving their country.

In our ignorance, we've forgotten the lessons of the past and grown apathetic about America's place in the world. Patriotism—another word for pride in America—has become a dirty word. During the 2014 World Cup, MSNBC commentator Chris Hayes lamented the failure of many Americans to embrace soccer, explaining the important lessons that the game had to teach us. In celebrating the United States' loss to lowly Belgium, Hayes noted that the American aversion to soccer was *weirdly* tied to American exceptionalism (or maybe we just prefer baseball?). He giddily noted: "Part of embracing a truly worldwide competition is accepting the fact the U.S. cannot simply assert its dominance," Hayes said. "Turns out we have to play just like everybody else."

Though the United States has been eliminated, the competition will go on, Hayes said, and "some amazing football is going to be played."[10] To Hayes and his ilk, national pride is a crude notion from a bygone era. I'm sure those Belgians are thankful that American men from that bygone era landed in nearby France, and sacrificed their lives to help create a world where Europe gets to have multiple soccer teams, rather than just one that would play under a swastika banner, but maybe I'm just crazy. Or maybe Chris Hayes is an entitled brat.

Statements like Hayes's are not unique among liberals today, but this is a rather new phenomenon. The American Left and Right have always had a different perspective on how to best organize America, but when I grew up, we had a shared understanding of our common enemy, socialism in its most extreme form: communism. Both parties recognized that the Soviet Union was an Evil Empire, the antithesis of the United States, a system that could not allow for freedom of religion, expression, or speech, where people lined up to get scraps from a bread line and political dissidents were sent to far-off prison camps (gulags) to be tortured or to freeze to death. In 1963, Democratic President John F. Kennedy visited Berlin, the city where the free world and the Iron Curtain were divided by a massive wall that would one day come tumbling down. In a speech that would become famous, Kennedy noted:

> There are many people in the world who really don't understand, or say they don't, what is the great issue between the free world and the Communist world. Let them come to Berlin. There are some who say that communism is the wave of the future. Let them come to Berlin. And there are some who say in Europe and elsewhere we can work with the Communists. Let them come to Berlin. And there are even a few who say that it is true that communism is an evil system, but it permits us to make economic progress. *Lass'sie nach Berlin kommen.* Let them come to Berlin.[11]

After nearly thirty years and dozens of direct conflicts and proxy wars, carried by the sacrifice and commitment of American soldiers and leadership to freedom, that wall eventually came down. It was torn apart by East and West Germans eager to reunite, using hammers, pickaxes, and their bare hands. Similarly oppressive regimes in Poland, Romania, and Czechoslovakia would soon follow. It was a beautiful moment that should have assigned the doctrines of collectivism to the dustbin of history, and it was accomplished by Republicans and Democrats alike. The ghettos, poverty, and pollution we saw on the other side should have served as a reminder of the superiority of the American system. America isn't perfect, but here was clear evidence that it was light-years better than the alternative.

So what the heck happened?

We got complacent. We won the war and lost the peace. In the absence of an existential threat we let the loony liberals that had been confined to college campuses and American cities back out, and we sent our kids to college to be indoctrinated by them without giving them a proper frame of reference. Today our college campuses are full of students being told that American hegemony is a global evil. That American intervention in defense of global freedom is nothing more than imperialism. That the wages of American capitalism are not wealth and greater prosperity, but global warming. That free speech is not healthy, but the path to racism, sexism, and "microaggression." Since the Cold War ended, we've had multiple generations of college students spoon-fed this crap, and the chickens are coming home to roost.

Take New York City. New York City may be liberal, but it's also the beacon of American capitalism and the home of the Statue of Liberty. It's the city that never sleeps, and has long rewarded the entrepreneurial spirit and attracted those who understand the old saying, "If I can make it there, I'll make it anywhere." Today, however, that city is governed by confirmed Leftist Bill de Blasio. This man believes that the notion of working hard to "make it there," or anywhere, is a farce—along with the American Dream. De Blasio spent his youth supporting Nicaragua's radical Marxist Sandinista guerillas. He honeymooned in Cuba, in violation of America's travel ban, because what could be more romantic than a socialist island prison? Perhaps de Blasio didn't notice the thousands of Cubans stringing together anything that floats in hopes of escaping, risking their lives on the ninety-mile drift to America.

Nationally, it's worse. Bernie Sanders is treated by the youth of America as a rock star. Bernie Sanders, the Woodstock-era hippie who spent his entire adult life making excuses for America's enemies. Today Bernie refers to himself as a "Democratic socialist," but in his younger years, the Senator from Vermont honeymooned in the Soviet Union, at a time when the regime was starving its citizens, torturing dissidents, and pointing nuclear warheads at the United States. The Soviet trip was originally scheduled as a "sister cities" program between Burlington, Vermont (Sanders was mayor), and Yaroslavl, a town 160 miles north of Moscow. During the 2016 primaries, socialist Bernie Sanders spoke to record crowds, galvanizing college campuses across the country. He pitched a radical departure from the American way, demanding that we transform our country into a Scandinavian socialist paradise, decrying the pursuit of wealth and pitching a dismal future where Americans born into a particular social class are condemned into that particular social class and can advance only by the good graces of government. Free college! Free health care! Free everything! The support received by someone who should have been dismissed as a fringe candidate is tragic. It shows just how much the radical Left has infiltrated even the mainstream Democratic party. It's telling—and terrifying—that one of their top leaders, Democratic National Committee Chair (and Florida congresswoman) Debbie Wasserman Schultz found herself unable to articulate the difference between a Democrat and a socialist.[12] This would no doubt alarm many of the patriotic Democrats like President Kennedy and Washington Senator Henry "Scoop" Jackson who helped the United States face down and defeat Soviet communism.

The ground for this full-scale assault on our national pride was laid by the election of Barack Obama, which is quite ironic. The former Senator from Illinois arose from humble circumstances and a broken home to become the first African American President of the United States. In his farewell address, George W. Bush remarked on the enormity of this:

> Standing on the steps of the Capitol will be a man whose
> story reflects the enduring promise of our land. This is a
> moment of hope and pride for our whole Nation. And I
> join all Americans in offering best wishes to President-elect
> Obama, his wife Michelle, and their two beautiful girls.[13]

Obama's story was a uniquely American one. One would think that no one would appreciate that fact more than Barack Obama, but from the beginning he's sought nothing more than a fundamental transformation of our country, and evinced a total disregard for the values that make it unique. The President, like many young Americans, is a product of his environment. Obama cut his teeth in places where love of country is considered a quaint, if not dangerous notion. He was schooled in the radical, blame-America-first Chicago church of Reverend Jeremiah Wright, the academic circles of the Ivy League, and the company of decrepit former revolutionaries like Weatherman Bill Ayers, reading Marxist books like Howard Zinn's *A People's History of the United States* that paint America as the imperialist scourge of the earth. It's no wonder that he ran on the promise of a fundamental transformation of America. When you've spent your whole life being told by everyone around you that there is nothing exceptional about America, maybe you start to believe it, despite all evidence to the contrary.

Some people have noticed his lack of pride in his country, and they've been sternly rebuked. When President Obama's patriotism was challenged by former New York City Mayor Rudolph Giuliani, the President responded: "I love my country enough to criticize it. To help make it better. To help it adapt to the times so that it may never perish." As *The Federalist's* David Harsanyi remarked at the time, "if you believe the ideals of the American Founding are expendable or malleable, if you believe they can be abandoned to adapt to contemporary crises, then you obviously don't believe that they're exceptional."[14] For their part, Obama's defenders suggest he's merely updating those ideas, which are too antiquated for the challenges that face America today. In previous generations, those ideas that Obama and his friends believe are so antiquated were good enough to end slavery, get America through the Civil War, assimilate millions upon millions of immigrants, and defeat Nazism and communism, and bring an end to Jim Crow, but they're useless for the ideas Obama has planned. They need updating.

Take, for instance, the First Amendment. In a recent poll, 51 percent of Democrats supported its repeal.[15] Or maybe it's just that Obama can't appreciate the staying power and universality of the American ideal.

Obama's disregard for America's unique place in the world is evident in the way he deals with foreign nations. Whether President Obama likes it or not, Ronald Reagan had it right when he noted that "the leadership of the free world was thrust upon us two centuries ago . . . we are indeed, and we are today, the last best hope of man on earth." America is the world's first experiment in liberty, and its most experienced opponent of tyranny, and the world is a better place for our global leadership, no matter what your college history professor says. Throughout its history, America has stood on the side of free people, and Presidents have had no problem with calling our enemy our enemy.

In the modern liberal mind-set, our enemies are our enemies because of *our* provocation. The history of United States' global engagement is one of oppression to the modern American liberal. As such, the United States has gone on a global apology and conciliation tour, and we're giving away the store. Where we used to make common cause with liberal democracies in pursuit of global freedom, our long-standing Democratic allies in Great Britain and Israel are persona non grata. Israel is our longest standing and only Democratic ally in the Middle East. Yet when they're beset by terrorism, this administration responds by drawing a moral equivalence between the actions Israel takes to defend her people and the terrorist attacks carried out by their enemies against Israeli civilians.[16] While the Obama administration demands restraint and throws criticism at America's liberal Democratic friends, he offers the benefit of the doubt to a totalitarian regime in Iran that openly chants "death to America" and finances global terrorism dedicated to harming our interests.

President Obama displayed an astonishing lack of pride when he embarked on his famous "apology tour" around the world shortly after getting elected. He told a French audience that

America had "shown arrogance and been dismissive, even derisive"[17] toward Europe. He told an audience in Cairo in 2009 that "America does not presume to know what is best for everyone,"[18] in a speech optimistically titled "A New Beginning" that was supposed to mend fences and build bridges between America and the Arab world.

Oops.

Since then, the Middle East has been engulfed in chaos—governments crumbled in the Arab Spring, American diplomatic and security personnel were slaughtered in Benghazi, ISIS continues a reign of terror over the wide sections of territory it holds, and Syria is mired in a civil war that has also roped in Russia and Iran. In a 2015 tally, *Breitbart News* found that fully half of the terror groups on the State Department's Foreign Terrorist Organization list have roots in the Arab world.[19] So much for new beginnings—unless, of course, you count the disastrous nuclear deal with Iran.

The Left's failure to recognize the threat of radical Islam, posed by enemies in many forms from ISIS to Iran, has its own roots in their inherent lack of pride. A feeling of shame, a supposed duty to remind the world, as Obama did, that "America does not presume to know what is best for everyone," is what has led them to turn a blind eye and willfully ignore legitimate threats. And as a result, ISIS has grown and flourished, and has inspired senseless violence not only in Europe, but on our own shores as well. And yet, as Texas Senator Ted Cruz has pointed out, "President Obama . . . literally will not utter the words 'radical Islamic terrorism' and as matter of policy, nobody in the administration will say the words 'radical Islamic terrorism.' "[20] The President's fellow Leftists, including his would-be successors, have an almost religious devotion to avoiding that phrase. They're afraid it somehow indicts all Muslims, even American Muslims, when it does not. In fact, a 2011 Pew survey found that about half of U.S. Muslims actually thought there should be *more* condemnation of extremism by their own clerics.[21] Genuine pride, not manufactured political correctness, will save us. Unfortunately, among some of our leaders that kind of pride is in short supply.

Don't panic. Well, okay, panic. But know this: There's still hope. Many Americans remain deeply concerned, and unapologetically proud of the country we grew up in. I wouldn't be where I am today if I had grown up in any other country but America. It's that simple. I still get a shiver sometimes when I hear a rendition of "The Star-Spangled Banner" and really let those words sink in. I'm touched when I think that the author of "God Bless America," Irving Berlin, was one of the eight children of Russian Jews who came to this country with absolutely nothing. He knew God blessed America because he knew how precious it was to become a part of it. The less fashionable term for this pride of country is, of course, patriotism, the belief in America as an exceptional nation, "the last best hope of man on earth."

I never forget that, not for a minute. That's hard to do when there's a giant reminder staring you in the face every day at work.

I've been in a lot of offices of people who've done well, and the walls are covered with pictures of themselves. Here they are smiling at you from a magazine cover, there they are gripping-and-grinning with someone even more famous than themselves. Okay, I admit, I've got a few pictures like that (though most of mine are of my family). However, the most prominent thing hanging in my office is a gigantic American flag. It takes up an entire wall. It's there partly out of pride, partly because it's so beautiful to look at, but it's also a reminder. It's a reminder that I got to where I am because of this country and the opportunities it provides.

A NATION MUST HAVE BORDERS

Those of us who have pride in this magnificent country know how important it is to defend what it means to be an American.

Hundreds of thousands of people over countless generations have died for the privilege of American citizenship.

Why did Donald Trump gain such traction in the 2016 campaign? Because he understood this privilege better than any other candidate. A nation must have respect for its borders and its laws or it is not a nation. Doesn't seem too complicated, does it?

I'm sure you've heard it said time and time again: "The United States is a nation of immigrants." And that's true. We all came from somewhere. My own family came from Sweden and Italy.

In a perfect world, where entrepreneurship and drive and tolerance was something every human being from Jakarta to Jalalabad to Juárez has in ample quantity, people would come to America from all over the world and, once they got here, work their hardest to make a better life for themselves and their families. In turn, that would make the country a better place, too. Unfortunately, we don't live in a perfect world. Because we live in the real world where men aren't angels and where selflessness isn't the norm, we have laws. Laws are supposed to keep us safe and keep the whole engine of American life running efficiently. If we don't like a law, we use the democratic process to change it or get rid of it altogether.

We fight back against bad laws at the ballot box. Nobody understands that better than Nancy Pelosi. She and her Democrat-led Congress passed the monstrosity known as Obamacare on Christmas Eve, 2009, giving Americans the mother of all bad Christmas presents. The following year, in the midterm congressional elections, the Democrats were voted out of the majority in the House of Representatives and Pelosi lost her Speaker's gavel. Republicans won in a landslide, and retook the Senate in 2014. While congressional Republicans are working to get rid of Obamacare, repealing it remains unlikely as long as President Obama—or a fellow Democrat—holds the White House. That's why the 2016 election is so important.

Obamacare is a classic example of a bad law that dedicated

citizens and their representatives are working hard to change. The fight against the government takeover of health care—in Washington, in the courts, and at the grassroots level—is proof that Americans value the democratic process on which our nation was founded. Respecting the law of the land—even if you don't agree with it and are actively working to change it—is a cornerstone of responsible citizenship.

Think about that phrase—"law of the land." Pretty simple, isn't it? It means that American laws cover American territory. And where does that territory begin? On our borders. Borders make a nation sovereign, and a nation has a right to control who can and can't cross those borders. Every nation of immigrants is still a nation of laws, including immigration laws. And if respecting the law of the land is part of being a good citizen, then how can you be a good citizen of a country if you violate its laws by entering it illegally in the first place?

The idea that a sovereign nation should have and enforce its own borders should not be a radical one. At least, it wasn't always. Recently, though, big business interests, looking for an easy source of cheap labor, have leaned on politicians from both parties to make our borders more porous, and to relax penalties on the millions of illegal immigrants already here.

Of course, they find willing allies on the Left. Liberal Democrat Senator Chuck Schumer of New York has lectured on the need to pass a "comprehensive" immigration reform bill in Congress "for the good of America, for the good of the 11 million living in the shadows, for the good of the industries and things like that."[22] "The industries" are definitely behind the idea, with the U.S. Chamber of Commerce—often a Right-leaning organization—reminding us that more immigration "would boost economic growth, create jobs, and spur innovation and entrepreneurship," not to mention "renew America's legacy of being an open and welcoming country where anyone who works hard can achieve his or her dreams."[23]

With the Chamber throwing its influence around, some Republicans are jumping into the Left's boat on this issue. Four Republican Senators joined Schumer and three other Democrats to form the "Gang of Eight," which introduced legislation in 2013 that would have meant more immigration and legalization for the illegal immigrants already here.

The legislation ultimately failed, and it's not hard to see why. Simply put: The American public doesn't want fewer restrictions on immigration, in fact, they want more. A 2015 Gallup poll found that 60 percent of Americans were dissatisfied with the country's current immigration levels, an increase from the year before.[24] The latest American Values Survey from the Pew Research Center saw 69 percent supporting the idea that the nation should "restrict and control people coming to live in our country more than we do now." And that thinking cut across racial and ethnic lines: 72 percent of whites agreed, along with 66 percent of blacks and 59 percent of Hispanics.[25]

Leftists in Congress, with some allies from the Republican establishment, tried to force through the "Gang of Eight" immigration bill that further opened our borders and went against the wishes of most Americans. The Gang of Eight fiasco occurred in 2013, and was certainly responsible in part for what happened to the Senate the following year. A Reuters poll published in August 2014 found 45 percent of Americans in favor of reducing immigration, while only 17 percent were in favor of increasing it.[26] A few months later, that November, Americans went to the polls and kicked out the Democrat Senate majority that tried to further open up our borders.

Out-of-touch elites in Washington tried to tell Americans what was best for them, and this time, the voters fought back. When his pet immigration bill failed in the Senate, Chuck Schumer blasted "the tea party" and "folks from the hard right," who Schumer said blocked the bill because "they hate immigration, they hate immigrants."[27] Actually, as much as Senator

Schumer might not want to admit it, it's not just the "hard right." The polling clearly shows that a majority of all Americans are opposed to mass immigration. That's certainly not based on "hate"—not even close—just a desire to keep our country's borders sovereign and control who crosses them in order to come live among us. Yet that's what the Left does. If you don't agree with their policies, you're hateful and a bigot. They set themselves up as the only righteous ones in the room. That must be the last-ditch strategy of people who clearly can't win with persuasive arguments.

And some of the arguments for increasing immigration are out in left field. I mean *really* out there. Some academics even like to argue for open borders entirely. One of them, Professor Alex Tabarrok at George Mason University, argues that "all people should be free to move about the earth, uncaged by the arbitrary lines known as borders."[28] Oddly enough, *New York Times* columnist David Brooks once listed Dr. Tabarrok among "the most influential bloggers on the right."[29] I'm not sure what this says more about, Tabarrok or Brooks.

In any event, Tabarrok claims that "closed borders are one of the world's greatest moral failings but the opening of borders is the world's greatest economic opportunity." He gets even more flowery, asserting that "a planet unscarred by iron curtains is not only a world of greater equality and justice. It is a world unafraid of itself."[30] Apparently, when you spend enough time in the ivory tower, the concept of national sovereignty is reduced to nothing more than "scarring" the earth with "iron curtains." Who knew that every country on earth had been doing it so wrong for so long?

If anything, the lessons of more than a million migrants— mostly from the Middle East—trekking to relatively borderless Europe in a single year gives us a preview of a world without borders at all. The European Union nations were simply overwhelmed, to the point where, in January 2016, ABC News reported:

Denmark and Sweden tightened border checks . . . to
stem the flow of migrants coming in from Germany,
dealing fresh blows to the vision of a Europe without
national boundaries.[31]

And that doesn't even account for the crime wave that en-
sued. On the last day of 2015, hundreds of women in one German city, Cologne, were subject to sexual assaults by gangs of
foreign men, including "refugees." Initially, the local authorities, out of an insane dedication to the same kind of political
correctness the Left wants to implement here in America, tried
to suppress these reports.[32] In January 2016, a Swedish woman
working to aid refugees was stabbed by one of them—reportedly a
fifteen-year-old boy—and killed.[33] The French town of Calais
was forced to erect its own checkpoint to deal with a crime-
ridden refugee camp known as the "Jungle."

The 2015 migrant crisis significantly shook confidence in the
open-border system in Europe—and if one continent can't
handle it, things don't look good for a borderless world. People
will always want to leave areas fraught with conflict, strife, and
poverty for destinations offering peace, stability, and prosperity. That's just the way the world works. And if borders were to
suddenly disappear, the influx into all Western nations would
make the recent European migrant crisis look like a few folks
out for a quiet stroll.

That's not to say that America doesn't welcome those who
want to come to this country in search of a better life. This country welcomed my ancestors, as it did many millions of others.
In the great "melting-pot" tradition, people came from all over
the world over the course of hundreds of years and, with the skills
and talents they brought with them, helped to make this country what it is.

The problem, however, is that this tradition has changed in
the last few decades. As Reihan Salam of *National Review* points
out, "skilled immigrants have been very much in the minority

in the post–1965 era."[34] An influx of unskilled immigrants has led to more of these immigrants relying on taxpayer-funded public assistance programs, like welfare. Salam, citing data from the Center for Immigration Studies, notes that "immigrant-headed households are far more likely to make use of means-tested safety-net programs, such as Medicaid and SNAP, than are native-headed households." This is backed up by government data:

> Drawing on data from the Census Bureau's Survey of
> Income and Program Participation, [CIS] finds that
> 49 percent of immigrant-headed households access these
> programs (as opposed to 30 percent of native-born
> households), and that the share rises to 72 percent for
> immigrant-headed households with children.[35]

With the mass legalization of illegal immigrants pushed for by the Left, we can only expect these numbers to go up.

Unskilled foreign labor, even when it is acquired legally, is also a major threat to some of the most vulnerable American workers. That was a lesson learned the hard way by vegetable pickers for Hamilton Growers in Georgia. In 2010, a supervisor there told eighty of their workers: "All you Americans are fired." The year before, another group of workers, many of whom were African American, got an even harsher dismissal: "All you black American people, f★★★ you all . . . just go to the office and pick up your check."[36]

These comments were included in a BuzzFeed News investigation, which revealed that "many businesses go to extraordinary lengths to skirt the law, deliberately denying jobs to American workers so they can hire foreign workers." Their investigation focused on H-2 visas, temporary guest-worker permits. Companies are, according to the federal H-2 program rules, supposed to "make good-faith efforts to employ Americans" so that they only hire immigrants to "fill positions no

Americans want." The "Americans won't do these jobs" line is a classic fallacy among mass-immigration advocates. The reality of the H-2 program, however, is that companies exploit it to rig the system against American workers from the start:

> [C]ompanies across the country in a variety of industries have made it all but impossible for U.S. workers to learn about job openings that they are supposed to be given first crack at. When workers do find out, they are discouraged from applying. And if, against all odds, Americans actually get hired, they often are treated worse and paid less than foreign workers doing the same job, in order to drive the Americans to quit. Sometimes, as the government alleged happened at Hamilton Growers, employers comply with regulations by hiring Americans only to fire them en masse and hand over the work to foreign workers with H-2 visas.[37]

I know some folks claim that immigrants do these jobs because Americans won't. And yeah, there are plenty of lazy Millennials out there who refuse to work if they can't find a job that is "fulfilling" or coddles them to the degree they're accustomed to. They sure don't help make us look like a nation willing to work. The truth is, though, there *are* struggling American citizens out there who *do* need jobs, and need them badly. And they are the ones who should get priority over foreign workers. If this section of our legal immigration system, the H-2 visa program, ends up screwing over American workers, how would the situation be made better for them by legalizing millions of illegal immigrants? *Breitbart News* estimated that "foreign-born workers seized all newly-created jobs from 2000 to 2014." Maybe it's time to give hardworking Americans a shot.[38]

If businesses exploiting the law to hire foreign workers over Americans is a concern, so, too, are the policies exploited by illegal immigrant criminals that allow them to remain in the United States to exploit the policies. Illegal immigrant crime can be a touchy subject for a lot of people. I was reminded of that in July 2015 when Geraldo Rivera went after me for talking about the murder earlier that month of Kate Steinle in San Francisco.

Steinle was shot dead, and the accused murderer was one Juan Francisco Lopez-Sanchez, an illegal immigrant with a criminal record including seven felony convictions. Lopez-Sanchez had already been deported from the United States five times previously, but had returned and was free to walk the streets of San Francisco thanks to that city's "sanctuary city" policy.

Geraldo got upset, and accused me of "exploiting and sensationalizing," but in fact I was just trying to have a discussion about illegal immigrant crime. And as it turns out, that kind of discussion, whether it's on a TV show or a larger national conversation, is made difficult by the fact that data can be hard to come by. Fox News did an investigation, published in September 2015, which noted that "government agencies that crunch crime numbers are utterly unable—or unwilling—to pinpoint for the public how many illegal immigrants are arrested within U.S. borders each year."[39]

From their own research, the Fox investigation did reveal that "illegal immigrants are three times as likely to be convicted of murder as members of the general population and account for far more crimes than their 3.5-percent share of the U.S. population would suggest." By combing through data from a number of government agencies, Fox found "the estimated 11.7 million illegal immigrants in the U.S. account for 13.6 percent of all offenders sentenced for crimes," including 12 percent of murders, 20 percent of kidnappings, and 16 percent of drug-trafficking offenses.[40]

Data from 2011 estimated there were some hundreds of thousands of illegal immigrants in American prisons—some 55,000 at the federal level and 296,000 in state and local jails. According to the Fox report, "experts agree those figures have almost certainly risen, although executive orders from the Obama administration may have changed the status of thousands who previously would have been counted as illegal immigrants."

Sanctuary cities only make horrific crimes like the murder of Kate Steinle more likely. And because of their commitment to more and more immigration, the Left wants to keep these policies in place. San Francisco's liberal leaders want to maintain their sanctuary policy, and Democrats in the Senate blocked a bill in October 2015 that would have weakened those policies nationwide.[41]

The liberal push for sanctuary cities arguably comes from *lack of pride*. It's almost as if sanctuary city policies are designed to lessen some massive chunk of guilt, to right some of America's supposed "wrongs" even at the expense of our laws, our sovereignty, and, in some cases, even the lives of our citizens.

These are the real-life consequences of our loss of national pride. If we are no longer proud of our nation, than what is the point of enforcing our borders? If we don't think that becoming an American citizen is special—even exceptional—any longer, why bother trying to control who gets in and who doesn't? National pride certainly flies in the face of the "open borders" philosophy.

It's not too late, though. America can still be a shining city on a hill—not just for those who want to come here, but for those who live here already. I've always loved that term, and I think remembering its meaning is the key to restoring our national pride. The phrase was first used by the pilgrim John Winthrop, aboard the ship *Arbella,* en route to what would become the Massachusetts Bay Colony, in reference to what would eventually become Boston: "We must always consider that we shall be as a city upon a hill, and the eyes of all people are upon us." Winthrop seemed to know that these settlers were embarking on a radical experiment, and laying the foundation of a nation that would be unlike any other that came before it. He knew that the entire world would be watching. The pilgrims were some of the first of many immigrants to see the New World, which would eventually become the United States, and, for generations after, the idea of America as a beacon of freedom and opportunity persuaded immigrants from all over the globe to flock to the United States, often with nothing more than the clothes on their back, in pursuit of liberty and prosperity.

The "city on a hill" rose to relevance again when President Kennedy addressed the Massachusetts legislature in 1961. In the aftermath of World War II, America had emerged as one of two global superpowers, and a Cold War to decide its fate was underway. Kennedy used it to note the awesome responsibility that America's unique history conferred upon us as a people:

I have been guided by the standard John Winthrop set before his shipmates on the flagship *Arbella* three hundred and thirty-one years ago, as they, too, faced the task of building a new government on a perilous frontier. "We must always consider," he said, "that we shall be as a city upon a hill—the eyes of all people are upon us." Today the eyes of all people are truly upon us—and our govern-ments, in every branch, at every level, national, state and local, must be as a city upon a hill—constructed and inhabited by men aware of their great trust and their great responsibilities. For we are setting out upon a voyage in 1961 no less hazardous than that undertaken by the *Arbella* in 1630. We are committing ourselves to tasks of statecraft no less fantastic than that of governing the Massachusetts Bay Colony, beset as it was then by terror without and disorder within. History will not judge our endeavors— and a government cannot be selected—merely on the basis of color or creed or even party affiliation. Neither will competence and loyalty and stature, while essential to the utmost, suffice in times such as these. For of those to whom much is given, much is required.[42]

Kennedy delivered this message at a time when freedom was endangered around the globe, as a communist Soviet Union radically opposed to the freedom of speech, religion, and commerce was a true existential threat. Standing up to a force so hostile required a national commitment that was impossible without a great national sense of pride.

More than twenty years later, a President who was a product of that era, who grew up with great admiration for Kennedy, made that phrase his own, and immortalized it. It was 1989 and communism was on death's door. Ronald Reagan's commitment to markets and human freedom had put the final nail in the coffin of the Soviet Union, and the country was riding high. The Iron Curtain was about to fall. The world was about to change dramatically.

Reagan's farewell address is often remembered as a celebration of America, and it was, but it was also a warning. Reagan painted a picture of America as "a shining city on a hill . . . a tall proud city, built on rocks stronger than oceans, windswept, God blessed, and teeming with people of all kinds, living in harmony and peace . . . with free ports, humming with commerce and creativity."[43] It's an image so breathtaking that it makes it easy to forget the rest of Reagan's speech. The image was meant to remind Americans not only what our country was, but also how precarious that condition was. He wanted us to know how fleeting freedom could be if we lost our sense of pride in it. Reagan was born of the Greatest Generation, people among whom national pride was ubiquitous, who reinforced it in schools and media and who appreciated those who fought for freedom in World War II and Korea. At the end of the Cold War, Reagan seemed to sense that a change was afoot. He saw a pop culture that was ambivalent or hostile to America's place in the world, and a generation of parents who were perhaps less enthusiastic about American ideals than the previous generation. In closing his address, he challenged Americans to restore that pride and patriotism, referencing the sacrifices of those who had fought and died on Omaha Beach and the pilgrims who came here seeking religious freedom, and what the promise of America meant to those people. Reagan asked us to remember, issuing the profound warning that "if we forget what we did, we won't know who we are." He urged American parents to reinforce those ideals at the dinner table, and American children to make sure they did.

There's still time for us to heed Reagan. There's still every reason to have pride in this great nation. As bad as things may seem, I'm encouraged by the hardworking Americans I meet every day. I'm encouraged by the members of our armed forces, the men and women who voluntarily put themselves in harm's way to keep us safe; the innovators and entrepreneurs, whose pursuit of the American Dream creates products that make our lives better. I'm excited about a Republican slate of candidates that included an African American who rose from abject poverty to become a world-renowned neurosurgeon, two Cuban American Senators whose parents fled totalitarianism and worked menial jobs so that their children could have a better life, and a woman who rose from the secretary pool to become the CEO of a Fortune 100 company. Whatever you may think of Ben Carson, Ted Cruz, Marco Rubio, and Carly Fiorina, their life stories all stand as a reminder that despite the insistence of the radical Left, we must continue to protect the American Dream, or we'll lose it forever. Now is the time to rise up to protect what we have left.

9. PROVIDENCE

noun prov·i·dence \'prä-və-dəns

(1.) divine guidance or care

(2.) God conceived as the power sustaining and guiding human destiny
—Merriam-Webster's definition

(1.) foolish beliefs that intrude on the proper functioning of the State

(2.) "opiate of the masses"—Marx
—A Leftist's definition

I have lived, Sir, a long time; and the longer I live, the more convincing proofs I see of this truth, that God governs in the affairs of men. And if a sparrow cannot fall to the ground without his notice, is it probable that an empire can rise without his aid?

—BENJAMIN FRANKLIN TO THE CONSTITUTIONAL
CONVENTION, 1787

One of the lowest moments in recent American times was when ISIS sympathizers stormed a Christmas party in San Bernardino, California, and unleashed a hell storm of bullets on Jews, Christians, and nonbelievers alike who had gathered joyfully and respectfully to celebrate one religion's annual heralding of "Peace on Earth." Maybe that's not your religion. Maybe that's not what you believe. Yet when more than a quarter of the world's population gets together every year to celebrate the arrival of a Savior who preaches tolerance and understanding and love and peace, it seems pretty out of whack to find offense in that.[1] However, that is precisely what Tashfeen Malik and Syed Rizwan Farook did, carrying out the worst terrorist attack on American soil since the 9/11 attacks on New York City, Washington, and in the skies above Shanksville, Pennsylvania.[2] With fourteen dead and more than a dozen gravely injured, the meticulously planned atrocity—on the heels of a larger and more devastating attack in the streets of Paris—confirmed what most Americans already knew: We are under attack from radical Islamic terrorists and we have been for a very long time. This attack in particular had roots in Saudi Arabia and was only carried out because of a disastrous immigration system and a refusal of the American government to take the threat seriously and conduct comprehensive background checks on the people streaming into this country from dangerous places around the world. These places are teeming with people who routinely vow to kill Americans—innocent men, women, and children—and sacrifice their own lives in an effort to destroy the United States of America and suicide bomb the entire peaceful, religiously tolerant civilized world back into the Dark Ages. That is their only aim. They will stop at nothing to achieve it. And the vast majority of Americans understand this. Except one, it seems.

Before the bodies had been cleared from the Christmas party in San Bernardino, President Obama took to the airwaves. Not to condemn radical Islamic terrorism, the motive investigators were quick to identify. Not to declare that America would fight and destroy this enemy. Rather, President Obama gave another one of his halting, disappointed-in-America speeches in which he used the terrorist attack to press an old, failed, partisan political agenda: gun control.

"We see the prevalence of these kinds of mass shootings in this country and I think so many Americans sometimes feel as if there's nothing we can do about it," he said in his signature tone of exasperation.[3]

So: America has just been attacked by radical Islamist jihadists and our President once again sees something wrong with

America. We have somehow failed to do something about "these kinds of mass shootings in this country." In the days and weeks to follow—even after he could no longer deny that this was a terrorist attack—President Obama and his allies in the Democratic Party never relented in using the San Bernardino dead as a ploy to push gun control. Even as Americans flooded gun stores to buy guns and stock up on ammo, as they often do after attacks like this. Gun-store owners reported something unusual this time, however. A huge number of these customers were first-time gun owners.[4] These Americans had given up on their President and their government to fight the war against radical Islamic terrorists. So, like every generation of great Americans before them, they decided to fight it themselves. And they bought more guns.

Adding grave insult to great injury, the Left not only shilled their daffy and doomed political agenda on guns, they also went on an unprecedented media campaign to attack religion and the millions of Americans who wept for their lost and wounded citizens in San Bernardino, those good people who fell to their knees and prayed to God that they would be comforted. These good people prayed for the dead, the survivors, and the families. Some even prayed for the perpetrators, in hopes their souls just might recognize the wickedness of their actions.

"GOD ISN'T FIXING THIS" blared the headline from the *New York Daily News*. "Prayers aren't working," the paper needled.[5]

Burrowing their heads in the same sand as President Obama, the Leftist paper went on a crazy partisan rant, blaming Republicans as "cowards who could truly end gun scourge."

This childish politicization of a terrorist attack from this particular newspaper is pretty amazing, considering that the *Daily News* supposedly serves readers in a city that witnessed the single worst terrorist attack ever on American soil. You would think they might belittle terrorism and have the decency not to use the deaths of fourteen innocents and serious wounding of dozens more simply to advance some partisan saw.

I could not help thinking of what a cruel and thoughtless attack on my faith this was as a devout Christian who prays every day and believes deeply in the power of prayer. It was as if the newspaper said my God is not real. Or God is dead. Or that my prayers are empty. Tell me, how is that *Daily News* cover and the onslaught of copycat messages that zapped around the Internet not at the very least the equivalent of drawing a picture of Muhammad? How is it not an insult a thousand times worse for Christians like me to be told that my prayers are meaningless? Would such an insult justify me donning a suicide bomb vest and walking into the newsroom of the *Daily News* and blowing it up? Would this kind of vile insult to the most important thing in my life—my very faith—justify my murdering fourteen people? Of course, I am being ridiculous and would never dream of such a thing. The reason is because—like the vast majority of Christians and religious Americans—I do not care the slightest whit what the *New York Daily News* does to amuse itself. The paper is such a sad irrelevancy that it just doesn't matter. My faith is so much greater and more important than some silly rag of a paper. And maybe, just maybe, there is a lesson in that for radical jihadists, who take such deadly affront to every little slight to their religion.

The radical Left has no problem defending radical Islam at every turn, and yet their open disdain for Christians and religious faith is apparent in every aspect of American life today. Hollywood, the mainstream media, Madison Avenue all display hostility toward Christians, especially those who adhere to their faith with genuine ardor. Politicians like President Obama and House Democratic Leader Nancy Pelosi occasionally flaunt their Christianity with the grace and tenor of clanged cymbals and banged gongs. Yet faith is almost always used as some kind of political shield. Pelosi usually brings up her Catholic faith when talking about her support for abortion. She fails to mention, however, that the Vatican has instructed priests to deny her communion until she reverses her decades-long advocacy for abortion.[6] Obama, too, isn't much of a churchgoer but is quick to deploy religious arguments to further his political agenda on, say, Obamacare. And, famously, Obama was a member of the politically connected and powerful Trinity United Church in Chicago for twenty years while it served his community organizing purposes. However, once the church's longtime pastor Reverend Jeremiah Wright became a political liability, Obama dropped the church like a stone. I do not mean to question Obama's or Pelosi's own personal faith, but it is striking how they seem to only deploy it when it serves their political purposes. It's almost like they belong to the United Church of Democratic Politics. Whatever the case, their stewardship as the most powerful leaders of the Democratic Party has done much to advance the hostile Leftist agenda to undermine the Christian faith.

LIBERAL RELIGIOUS BIGOTRY

It really is hard to comprehend how anyone could possibly object to churches and other faith institutions when you consider all the great ways these organizations benefit society and people. This statement is especially true when it comes to poor people and minorities. Given the overwhelming body of evidence showing how much they help poor people and minorities, it is safe to say at the very least that people who are against churches and other good faith institutions do not care too terribly much about the plight of poor people or minorities. Yet, it is the militant Left—the very people who proclaim most loudly to care about the poor and minorities—that despises religion in all its forms. And their deepest hatred is reserved for that most evil of all—the Christian church. To understand this special form of bigotry, you have to understand that theirs is not a theological argument. It is an argument about power. They cannot really make a theological argument (except that any structure of right and wrong that makes people feel guilty is bad). Even this argument is flawed. I know this because I know something about guilt.

I carried guilt over a single childhood misdeed for several decades. Where I went to kindergarten, whenever someone had a birthday, all of the kids in the class would bring a small gift for the birthday boy or girl. One day, a girl named Ninette Schiller was turning five. And I forgot. I showed up at school with no gift, and felt terrible. I was the only kid who hadn't brought a gift for Ninette. What was I going to do? Next to me sat a boy named Sander Kaplan, who had brought in $4 for Ninette's gift. Before it came time to give our presents, Sander went to the bathroom, leaving the $4 on his desk. While he was gone— God help me—I stole it. I gave Ninette the money as my present, and she was thrilled. Meanwhile, Sander had come back, found his money gone, and was inconsolable. He cried for an hour. I immediately felt like a real creep, and remembered him crying for forty years. It was the only time I've ever stolen anything in my life. Recently, I decided to use the great resources we all have at our fingertips through the Internet to do something about it. Two years ago, I tracked down Sander Kaplan on Facebook. I reached out to him, confessed my decades-old crime, and apologized. I couldn't have guessed Sander's reaction: He didn't even remember! And here I'd been living with the guilt from that dumb, childish action for so long. Yet I think that guilt, as part of my faith as a whole, helped keep me on the straight and narrow after that.

That kind of faith isn't something you can expect a radical Leftist to understand. The reason they don't like the church is because church and God represent a threat to their desire to build something else (a massive government) that places them in power. And totalitarian power is what they want. And there is no room in a totalitarian regime for God or church. God and churches pose an existential threat to the socialist paradise the Left wants to build in the land of the free.

Which is why the Left is so intent on destroying those institutions. It's why the virtues of religion are deemed "trigger words" on college campuses, where shouting mobs of adolescent tin-pot despots shriek and complain about the "anguish" of capitalist, American norms. Religious belief is banned in communist regimes because the whole ideology of collectivism is to substitute faith in government for faith in the Almighty. It is rooted in Karl Marx's famous phrase that religion is the "opiate of the masses."[7] And President Obama made clear his contempt for religion with his now infamous statement about Middle Americans bitterly clinging to "religion" (and guns) to solve their problems. Seven years later, Obama returned to the topic of these bitter Americans in an interview with National Public Radio, just before jetting off on the taxpayer's dime for a two-week vacation in Hawaii.

"Particularly blue-collar men have had a lot of trouble in this new economy, where they are no longer getting the same bargain that they got when they were going to a factory and able to support their families on a single paycheck," the President said, explaining how real-estate mogul Donald J. Trump is "exploiting" voters. "You combine those things and it means that there is going to be potential anger, frustration, fear. Some of it justified but just misdirected."[8]

In the interview, Obama went on to say that his "unique demographic" and accusations that he is a closet Muslim exacerbate the frustrations of these "blue-collar men." In other words, they were unhappy not because the economy Barack Obama lorded over for seven years stinks and wages stagnated and Obamacare destroyed the forty-hour workweek. The *real* problem, Obama suggested, is that they are unhappy because of their own racism and bigotry. Well, America, you can't say you were not warned! It sure would be nice, though, if the President spent more time fixing the economy and less time studying demographics.

As bad as the President has been for the economy and representative democracy, he has been a great general in the Leftist war on religion. Consider two of the biggest fights the President has waged during his presidency: Obamacare and gay marriage. Is it just a coincidence that these two Leftist utopian mirages grind away at two of the most fundamental cornerstones of the Christian church? Whether or not you believe that contraceptives destroy life, we can all at least agree that the single biggest church on the planet stalwartly believes that contraceptives amount to abortion. And, therefore, for Obamacare to force Catholic taxpayers to spend their tax dollars violating their most precious religious tenet is, at the very least, depriving them of their religious liberty. Also, it is a sick and callous way to punish believing, faithful Catholics in the most inhumane and degrading way, an act of genuine disrespect against them from their own government. Gay marriage is another topic on which reasonable people may reasonably disagree. Yet, like Obamacare, it is not enough to just let disagreements lie. And I have a strong suspicion that a major motivation behind pressing this issue is that, like Obamacare, the issue has tentacles that reach deep into the foundation of religion. After life, marriage and familial duty and fidelity are probably the most sacred tenets of the Christian church.

Few topics get more airtime from the pulpit than the importance of marriage and family. And, once again, the political issue of gay marriage directly confronts and undermines the clear teachings of the church when it comes to marriage and the formation of a family. And what's particularly interesting here is that President Obama himself was opposed to gay marriage when he got elected in 2008, stating his belief at that time that "marriage is between a man and a woman." But by the time 2012 rolled around, he not only reversed his political position on the matter, he also believed so fervently in his new position that he took the extraordinary step of declaring that he would summarily dismiss the duly enacted Defense of Marriage Act, the federal law that defined "marriage" as the union between one man and one woman. In effect, President Obama was basically forcing gay marriage on states—a violation of federal law—even if the states had individually declared gay marriage unlawful.[9] Sure, his dramatic road-to-Damascus conversion on gay marriage—or as he called it, his "evolution"—happened just in time for his reelection campaign, but it goes to show just how committed Leftists are about undermining the most cherished foundations of the church.

Barack Obama has presided over an administration that has been overtly hostile to people of faith, especially Christians. Yet as he prepares to leave office, I hope he's realized something. I hope he's realized that the God-fearing Americans he so callously dismisses as clinging to religion aren't going anywhere. Yes, President Obama: We are still clinging. We will continue to stand strong long after you have left the White House, just as people of faith have done since this nation's founding. And any of your fellow Leftists who hope to succeed you in office had better remember that, too.

MOST SACRED LIBERTY

When the American Founders invented religious liberty and unleashed it on the world over two hundred years ago, it literally sparked a bloody revolution. It was a radical concept that caused an upheaval so tectonic that the reverberations would eventually be felt in every corner of the globe. Not since Jesus Christ walked the streets of Jerusalem had rulers, tyrants, and despots on earth faced such an existential threat to their way of life, their way of rule, their absolute power. The Founders were, at once and all of them, some of the most piously religious men of their time, while also some of the most profoundly secular men of their time. They believed deeply that religious freedom was the first and most fundamental right not only because they passionately believed in their own right to practice their own religion in their own way, but also because they understood the flip side of that. They believed with equal passion that they did not have the right to force anyone else to practice their religion. It is a concept we take woefully for granted today. Yet at the time, it was a truly radical concept. It was unheard of. It was dangerous. It posed a threat to every king and every queen who ruled anywhere on the planet.

In a deeply personal way, it means I get to practice my Catholic faith however I see fit. It is strictly between God, my family, and me. My faith has sustained me through the darkest points of my life and kept me grounded during the highest joys. My faith is with me every moment I am awake and watches over me when I sleep. Every morning, on my way into work, at about 9:00, I step into St. Patrick's Cathedral on Fifth Avenue. It's quiet then. The air is still and heavy, and you can hear the echo of anyone else who is moving around in the church. Before long I'll be in the middle of a buzzing newsroom, or in meetings trying to put together a TV show where I'll have a loud, boisterous discussion with four other people. Yet, for those few minutes every morning, when I step into the cathedral and light a few candles, there is peace. That's why I never miss a day. Not once. I go to church every Sunday, too.

I consider myself devout, and I guess that comes from being raised that way and having spent years at Catholic school. However, I don't just pray because someone long ago told me that I should. I pray because I know what prayer can do. I don't pray for success. I don't pray for material gain. All I seek when I'm praying is confidence. Going on national TV every day has its challenges, just like any other job. Whatever else may be going on in my life, I have to tune that out and just do the show. Yet if I've been to the church that morning and lit candles, I know I can call upon the peace I felt in that moment and the confidence I get from my faith in God. That was my father's faith, too. And my mother's. And my sister's. And it has been tested many, many times. Cancer has stalked my family, as it has many others. My mother died of ovarian cancer. Seven years after her, my father died of pancreatic cancer. And just a year after that,

that same disease took my sister. Losing your parents is hard enough, but losing a sibling at that point in your life is devastating. Her passing was a shock to everyone. Yet she, Mom, and Dad had all prayed their entire lives—up until the end. Now, I pray for all of them. And I light candles for them every morning at St. Patrick's. It is something that so many of us in America take utterly for granted, but in many places all across the world, people are beaten, arrested, and killed for trying to practice their religion. Sometimes it is mob justice. Sometimes it is the government.

Obviously, going to church is a deeply beneficial routine for me, just as it is for my entire family. Just as it is for Christians everywhere. And, I imagine, just as practicing other faiths is deeply beneficial to the practitioners of those faiths. Prayer is a useful reminder that we're not in charge, that there's something bigger guiding our lives. That there's such a thing as providence.

This used to be a widely shared belief in America, not just something confined to Right-wing Bible-thumpers, as the media portrays us over and over again. The first Americans came here believing that providence had created a sanctuary for them across an ocean and in a new wilderness where they could practice their faiths as their consciences demanded and where they could build a society that conformed to their view of the Bible.

The benefits of faith freely practiced in a society go far, far beyond just the souls of those fed on Sunday morning. Countless studies have shown that churches provide vital services and positive influences for society.

"The American founders viewed churches as a central institution within American life, because religion provided the moral foundation of self-restraint and community awareness necessary for the success of republican self-government," writes University of Cincinnati Professor Andy Lewis, who has studied church influences on society for the Ethics & Religious Liberty Commission.

"Many believed that the American experiment would not

succeed without the moral training churches provided to citizens. Churches, surely, have contributed to the success of America by encouraging virtue, but social science research has also shown that churches provide direct and indirect economic and social benefits to communities."[10]

So not only do our churches feed our souls every Sunday, they also feed the hungry every other day of the week, no matter what their faith might be. In addition, churches for hundreds of years have seen broader, more secular education as a central mission. The more literate and educated people are, the better. This benefits not only the church, but also the country. After all, if the Founders believed in suddenly seizing the keys to the kingdom from the king and handing them over to the people, those people had damned well better be educated. And churches have been on the leading edge of that mission for centuries. Countless studies have shown that robust churches improve education, lower crime, encourage volunteer social services, and even promote good mental and physical health.

"The average religious individual lives seven years longer than the average nonreligious individual, and this increases to fourteen years for African American individuals," according to Andy Lewis. "Research by Johns Hopkins scholars shows that nonreligious individuals have increased risks of dying from cirrhosis of the liver, emphysema, arteriosclerosis, cardiovascular diseases, and suicide."[11]

If you notice, there is a pattern here. Churches help the larger communities in which they reside in a number of ways, and that help is not just free charity. Churches help by empowering people. They help by giving people control over themselves and their lives. They help people improve themselves so that they can stop doing things that hurt them and the people around them. Ultimately, the church teaches, nurtures, and encourages people so that they—quite literally—take control of their own destiny. And this was the central question faced by the Founders. How to take a citizenry that had been ruled by a king thousands of miles across an ocean and put them in charge. How could a citizenry be trusted to govern themselves? For the Founders, the single most important answer to that question was religious liberty. Only through freedom of religion would citizens embrace of their own free will the many virtues of religion and incorporate those virtues into their civic life while at the same time respecting the differing religious views of fellow citizens. So while the Founders clearly believed that no specific religion should be established or promoted by the federal government of the United States of America, they just as firmly believed that a free nation of self-governed individuals could not exist for one single day without a belief in God. Which is why our faith found its way into nearly all our national slogans, our currency, and our courtrooms. Religious liberty—rooted in a belief in God—is the keystone freedom that makes possible every other freedom we enjoy in America.

I often find myself wondering what Thomas Jefferson, James Madison, or George Mason would think if they were to land in America today and step out of their time capsule from more than two hundred years ago and see what their country has become. Read a week's worth of newspapers, maybe flick on the television and watch a week's worth of cable news. Surely, they would be in awe of so much. Can you imagine Benjamin Franklin surveying a television for the first time, looking behind the tube in search of the little people? We've come a long way since he first felt electricity coursing through his kite string.

It was clear to the Founders that in their quest to bring forth this new nation, they were not flying completely blind. Perhaps there was no earthly precedent; the American Experiment was, after all, just that—an experiment. Washington and Madison and Franklin and their comrades recognized that they were fulfilling a higher purpose. Even Jefferson, while not a Christian himself, believed in a higher power, and wrote in the Declaration of Independence that the American colonists were only seeking to claim the rights due to them under "the laws of nature and of nature's God." Our Founders were inspired by the philosophical principles of the Enlightenment—the movement that merged Judeo-Christian values with the concept of individual rights. The idea of creating a nation based on these principles was almost unheard of, but they considered it their duty to try. It was as if they viewed it as their destiny.

The idea of destiny has always been a source of inspiration in the American character. That's no accident. Through our history there has run the thread of fate. "Manifest Destiny" drove intrepid American pioneers to settle the far-flung corners of the country. Our founding was a part of a higher plan, as was the role we grew to play in the world. It was not by dumb luck that we fought and triumphed over the murderous ideologies of fascism and communism. Deep down, we know our country is still meant for great things. That's why it is so important to fight back against those who tell us that the hand of providence—divine inspiration—has no place in American life today (public or private). It's why we must fight against those who would deny our destiny.

The Founders would certainly be alarmed about how disastrously modern Leftists in America have perverted the First Amendment to the Constitution they crafted. To them, and to a great many regular Americans today, its intent would seem obvious and straightforward:

> Congress shall make no law respecting an establishment
> of religion, or prohibiting the free exercise thereof; or
> abridging the freedom of speech, or of the press; or the
> right of the people peaceably to assemble, and to petition
> the Government for a redress of grievances.[12]

The Founders wanted to put an end to the tyranny of punishing or harassing people for their political speech or the debates they had printed in the myriad publications of the day. Just as important, they wanted to put an end to the punishing or harassing of people who gathered peaceably to vent their grievances about the government. Yet the first and most important protection they listed was religious liberty. "Congress shall make no law respecting an establishment of religion." Very simple. However, in no way did that phrasing undermine the concrete fact that from the Declaration of Independence to the U.S. Constitution to the Bill of Rights, America was founded on the belief that our rights come directly from God. From the Declaration's assertion that the rights of individuals are "endowed by their Creator" to the motto "In God We Trust" that graces our currency today, the United States has never established a state religion but merely stated the obvious: Without God, our liberties vanish and we become subjects to other men all over again. Our Founders did not believe that learning the stories of the Bible amounted to the establishment of a state religion. And if a local town wants to erect a monument to the Ten Commandments in the courthouse square, why shouldn't they? Moses was our first lawgiver in recorded history. His visage properly graces the U.S. House of Representatives and the Supreme Court. To pretend that Moses or the Ten Commandments are just some religious talismans that can be easily discarded is the height of ignorance. It is to deny history and mock the rule of law that makes America the greatest country on earth. It denigrates the concept of justice under God that fervently protects the vulnerable and minority rights.

In my own past, I learned a valuable lesson about protecting the rights of the vulnerable while attending a Jesuit high school. One of our regular activities in gym class was trampoline practice. We'd jump onto the trampoline, bounce upward and land on a mat on the ground. There was one kid in my gym class—we'll call him Sid—who was a real wise guy. He was always mouthing off about something and got on everyone's nerves. So one day, during trampoline practice, I—and a couple of other guys—decided to pull a prank on him to teach him a lesson. When Sid jumped for the trampoline, we pulled the mat out of the way, so when he landed, he hit the floor. Luckily he wasn't hurt, but our gym teacher was livid about what happened. I took a beating for it—literally, because schools still did that back then. My rear end got paddled, and I firmly believed I was receiving nothing less than God's justice. God always provides for justice for everyone.

Yet to Leftists, religion is a source of *in*justice, not justice, and so it must be attacked. The ignorant Leftists who despise knowledge, history, and justice under God have prevailed in so many of their quests to obliterate any reference to God or basic history from the public square, and from society as whole. And in so doing, they have completely perverted the First Amendment into something that would be totally unrecognizable to the Founders. In today's America, the First Amendment somehow protects a woman's right to saunter around all the children and tourists in Times Square completely topless while also requiring the removal of a monument to the Ten Commandments from a courtroom in Alabama. In today's America, Tea Party groups are relentlessly and ruthlessly targeted by the Internal Revenue Service and unfairly taxed as punishment for their political beliefs. At this, the Founders would scratch their heads in disbelief and probably climb back into their time machine and return whence they came, out of fear for what the ignorant mob would do to them if they were discovered and their political beliefs became known.

One of the really great things about being an American is that you can be a Muslim or a Jew, a Christian or an atheist, a Wiccan or a Satanist, and yet no matter what you are, because you are an American, you are inherently blessed with rights and freedoms designed by our Founders, but indelibly bestowed by our Judeo-Christian Creator. No matter what you claim your faith to be, all Americans are created equal. Nobody can take that away. You are blessed with rights derived directly from God. It was a radical concept when the Founders unleashed it on the world over two hundred years ago. The idea that our rights come from God means that no king or government or church or theocratic despot can deprive us of our liberties without the consent of the people. Without this covenant, America ceases to exist. Without this most fundamental Judeo-Christian principle, freedom evaporates and the great beacon unto the world will be snuffed out. Death, tyranny, and darkness will be all that remains.

It was sometime back in the summer of 2014 when I pulled up the *Drudge Report* and I could not believe my eyes. There was the story. "ISIS SLEDGEHAMMERS JONAH'S TOMB."[13] Ever since President Obama had surrendered Iraq to the terrorists, those fanatics had been wreaking havoc, killing innocents, growing stronger, and spreading their sphere of hatred and fear farther and farther across the Middle East. Eventually, of course, their evil wickedness would reach deep into the civilized world and hit places like Paris and San Bernardino, California. Yet in 2014, ISIS was just getting going. And it was not enough to just kill the "infidels" and spread their message of terror and hate. They were obsessed with obliterating history—history that they wished to ignore or refused to believe. So they took sledgehammers to the tomb of the prophet Jonah, a historic site deeply revered by people of all faiths. Their reign of destruction erased thousands and thousands of years of precious history across the Middle East. In addition to Jonah's tomb, ISIS thugs took hammers, drills, and explosives to churches, mosques, and libraries across Iraq and into Syria. They tore down statues and smashed ancient and priceless antiquities—all of it irreplaceable. They took a sledgehammer to civilization.

"We have lost about 10 percent of our heritage," the director of Iraq's state board of antiquity and heritage told the media at the time. "ISIS has destroyed many statues and sold the rest."[14]

Others placed the scale of destruction at a far higher level.

But it was the destruction of the Tomb of Jonah that I found particularly shocking. Jonah is not just an important figure to Christians and Jews, but also to mainstream Muslims. Yet the terrormongers of ISIS wage war not only on Jews, Christians, and infidels, but also on truth and history and civility. It is something I cannot help thinking about when I watch the heavily funded Leftist groups hell-bent on tearing down America's most precious monuments and obliterating the very history and ideals that created the greatest country on earth, the most powerful beacon for liberty around the world.

OBAMA'S TWISTED LIBERTY

In 2015, the town of Bethlehem, New York, gave up. Tired of fighting all the legal battles, the town decided not to light up their "Merry Christmas" sign in the town named for the birthplace of Jesus.

"It boggles the mind the extent to which government entities overreact," Jeremy Tedesco, senior counsel with the conservative legal nonprofit Alliance Defending Freedom (ADF), told *The Washington Times*. "The thing is, putting up a 'Merry Christmas' sign is not illegal. It's just not."

The people of Bethlehem's betters in city hall thought differently, though. "It is the Town Attorney's analysis that it is better not to include signs," the town of Bethlehem said in a press release. "That way, we can avoid contentious litigation or having the Town thrust into controversy over whose sign shall be placed where, etc."

There is, literally, still no room in Bethlehem for a "Merry Christmas" sign.

It wasn't malice on the part of the local government, Jeremy Tedesco of the ADF pointed out. "I'm not saying they're doing this out of some kind of ill will," he said. "It's clearly a misunderstanding of the law. It's not helped by the fact that, yes, there are groups out there like the Freedom From Religion Foundation and the ACLU that will rattle sabers where they have no business rattling them. The other side definitely creates an atmosphere of fear for these officials."[15]

The only good news here is that outside of the ACLU and other radical Leftist organizations funded by huge special interest groups, most Americans understand the law and history better than the lawyers and self-ordained constitutional "experts." And they have the wisdom to know the importance of religion in society. After radical activists complained about "Christian privilege" because of a Nativity scene set up on a city park in Wadena, Minnesota, last year, the town dismantled it. Residents responded by erecting crèches in their own front yards. By Christmas day, the one single Nativity scene removed from a city park had spawned thousands in people's front yards all over town.

The angry Leftists are not content only trampling religious liberty and obliterating American history from education and the public square. Their task will not be complete until they have totally perverted the Founders' ideals for a free democratic republic. Not until they have entirely gutted self-governance will their job be finished. And nobody has done more—perhaps unwittingly—to advance the cause for these people than President Obama, whose understanding of religious liberty is seriously twisted. The President has been rebuked by the Supreme Court for his faint grasp of the Constitution more than a dozen times since he was elected to the White House. President Obama has been checked by the Supreme Court for overstepping his constitutional authority, misapplying the law, or simply not understanding the most basic fundamentals of the U.S. Constitution. He has been repudiated, *unanimously,* over a dozen times by the Supreme Court. So even the Supreme Court justices he picked for the high court concurred that their political benefactor was out of line. And the man was a constitutional scholar and law professor! No wonder our education system—especially our law schools—are such a disaster. No wonder law school graduates have such a hard time getting jobs when they've been "educated" by people like Barack Obama.

With his frail understanding of the Constitution and his

disregard for cherished tenets of freedom such as religious liberty, President Obama has done so much to dismantle American self-governance. I try to give him the benefit of the doubt that he doesn't really wish to destroy American freedom. Perhaps he just got caught up in the politically correct Leftist world and succumbed to the groupthink that they bully people into. Maybe he just got sucked up into the top echelons of higher education and fell prey to all the received wisdom spouted by academics. Columbia University and Harvard Law could brainwash the best of them. What I still cannot understand, though, is why President Obama takes it a whole step further and adds great insult to the grievous injury he does to religious liberty and American freedom.

When Pope Francis made his first visit to the United States, it was an historic event for Christians, especially Catholics. I realize this pope has stirred up some controversy wading into areas of debate that popes have traditionally left alone, but you have to give him credit—he has shined the spotlight on the Catholic faith, and it is not very often the Catholic Church gets positive coverage in the mainstream media. After he became pope, I noticed in my daily visits to St. Patrick's Cathedral a real uptick in the number of people in church. That result by itself is a good thing. Also, it is hard not to admire what a humble man—and humble pope—Francis has been. If anything, the more controversial aspects of Pope Francis—some of which I don't particularly agree with—only make a lot of us Catholics like him more. He makes us want to stick up for him and defend him and protect his right to have the courage of his convictions. Anyway, no matter what individual political disagreements we might have, there wasn't a single Catholic in America who wasn't excited to see Pope Francis visit the United States. He was going to be received by the President at the White House. It was a very big moment—literally, a once-in-a-lifetime moment for Catholics in America.

So how, exactly, does this President welcome Pope Francis to the White House? In a stunning display of hostility toward his honorable guest, President Obama arranged for a handful of people representing some of the thorniest hot-button issues to be inside the White House to greet the pope. He invited Simone Campbell, a nun who—unbelievably—is a proabortion activist. I cannot tell you how such a thing is even remotely possible or where the President found somebody like her. Imagine the hatred that must boil deep within to find such an offensive person to greet the pope at the White House. President Obama also invited retired Episcopal Bishop Gene Robinson to greet the pope. He became the first openly gay Episcopal bishop in 2003 after leaving his wife of fourteen years. He later made further history by becoming the first openly gay Episcopal bishop to divorce his gay partner in 2014. While Pope Francis has made abundantly clear that the Catholic Church remains open to everyone, he—and the church itself—remains opposed to gay marriage and, at the very least, sees divorce as a highly unfortunate outcome of any marriage. He once described gay marriage as Satan's "attempt to destroy God's plan." And yet, here is President Obama, dragging in a proabortion nun and an openly gay-married and twice-divorced Episcopalian bishop. How does such aggressively rude behavior not amount to bullying? How is this level of hostility toward the highest mortal leader of a massive worldwide church not viewed as religious bigotry? How is this anything but just downright hateful?

As if making a total mockery of Pope Francis's faith and his church's most revered religious beliefs wasn't enough, President Obama took it even one step further. He turned the pope's visit into a full-blown carnival by also including Mateo Williamson, a cross-dressing woman and former cochair of the DignityUSA Transgender Caucus.

Williamson says that though she now thinks of herself as a man, she continues to be attracted to males, according to *Breitbart*

News: "Today I identify as a gay man and before that was difficult to understand because I thought that in order to be transgender, in order to be a transgender male that I had to be attracted
to females but I never have throughout my entire life."[16, 17]

Just another hero, I guess. Turning something as momentous
and special for so many millions of Catholic Americans into a
three-ring circus shows a level of pettiness, disrespect, and
downright hostility to the people the President is supposed to
be serving and representing. It also showed a callous disregard
for the religious liberty on which America was founded. Yet
what President Obama did next was so deeply offensive and utterly inexplicable that it shows why so many people do not trust
him. It reveals why so many people make such outrageous accusations about the President being Muslim or having Muslim
sympathies or not having been born in America. I personally
do not believe any of these accusations, but I do understand
how this President's actions can invite such invective and dis-
trust.

A few days after President hosted His Holiness Pope Francis
in the White House and forced him to greet a proabortion nun,
a gay and divorced retired bishop, and a cross-dressing activist,
the Obamas hosted the leader of the largest, most powerful
communist country on the planet today. President Xi Jinping
maintains communist China's wretched human rights record
with deadly force.

Under the new Chinese President, "authorities have also unleashed an extraordinary assault on basic human rights and their
defenders with a ferocity unseen in recent years—an alarming
sign given that the current leadership will likely remain in power
through 2023," cited the Human Rights Watch.

"The government targets activists and their family members
for harassment, arbitrary detention, legally baseless imprisonment,
torture, and denial of access to adequate medical treatment," the
group reports.[18] In other words, they round freedom-seeking cit-

izens up and toss them in jail for no reason other than they seek to
be free. And then they die in jail.

Xi Jinping's government "has also significantly narrowed
space for the press and the Internet, further limiting opportunities for citizens to press for much-needed reforms," according
to Human Rights Watch. Even more troubling, the totalitarian
regime has a special animus toward Christianity.

"In 2014, the government stepped up its control over religion, with particular focus on Christian churches," the group
reported. "Between late 2013 and early July, the government
removed 150 crosses from churches in Zhejiang Province,
which is considered to be a center of Christianity."[19] Later that
year, the government sentenced a Christian pastor to twelve
years in prison—for being a Christian pastor.

So, just a couple days after Pope Francis was rudely dressed
down during an official White House visit over his religious beliefs, the head of a regime that represses religious liberty and
other human rights arrived for a visit. The man should be arrested for what he does to his own people. He should be sent to
a "re-education" labor camp to learn the precious value of religious liberty and civil rights. Yet how is Chinese dictator Xi
Jinping received by this President at this White House? Well,
with a lavish state dinner, of course. We served him wild mush-
room soup with black truffle (very expensive, by the way, even
when in season). He also chowed down on butter-poached
Maine lobster with spinach, shiitake, and leek rice noodle rolls,
along with grilled cannon of Colorado lamb with garlic fried
milk and baby broccoli. This is what your tax dollars pay for:
to host a guy like China's communist leader. And it came just
two days after the public humiliation of Pope Francis for his religious beliefs. The only hint of dissent for Xi Jinping's state
dinner might—just might—have been the faint rumbles of a
protest going on outside the White House gates where protesters had gathered to complain about China's horrid human rights

record. You can rest assured, though, that China's President did not see a glimpse of this protest. The White House had erected screens around the entire North Front portico to shield Xi Jinping's eyes from the unruly mob outside: to shield his eyes from the very specter of freedom.[20]

EPILOGUE

THE GREATEST VIRTUES OF THE
GREATEST GENERATION

The island nation of Vanuatu is an archipelago of eighty-two volcano-forged islands nestled deep in the South Pacific. It is some 1,000 miles east of northern Australia and 7,700 miles west of my hometown of Chicago. Today its many islands are home to a population of more than 250,000 people.

In 1943, the islands, then known as the New Hebrides, were the scene of savage fighting as the U.S. Navy and Marines fought island by island, inching steadily toward imperial Japan. The war had visited American soil with a surprise attack on Hawaii two years earlier. In an unprecedented burst of patriotism and collective sacrifice the United States mobilized for war almost overnight. Some of the Greatest Generation went East to the European theater to challenge Hitler's and Mussolini's fascist forces that controlled an entire continent; others went West to the Pacific theater to battle Japan's fearsome navy and kamikaze pilots. One of the men who went West was Eric Bolling. Then twenty years old, the navy airman is believed to have plunged into the sea off the coast of Vanuatu.

I never knew much about the man whose name I carry. By the time I was born, the earlier Eric Bolling, my uncle, was a distant memory, one of many thousands of young Americans who served his country in World War II and died in its defense. He was my father's older brother, and for whatever reason, Dad never much talked about him. Maybe he was too young to remember him. Maybe, like so many of that generation, he was taciturn and didn't feel the need to emote or wax eloquent about his family's war stories. Maybe his loss was too painful.

Many young Americans today feel no ownership of the Second World War, and no personal connection to the most epic and deadliest struggle between the forces of freedom and tyranny. Most of the brave men who fought in that pivotal conflict would now be nearly a century old. And so Millennials' eyes glaze over when they read about "the Greatest Generation" and what they sacrificed for us. And I'll confess at some points in my life, at least when I was a kid, I wasn't that different. I never knew my uncle, so I never truly felt his loss.

Over time, however, that started to change. Little by little I've come into possession of pieces of that young man's life that made him feel a little more real.

In January 1942, Eric Baltazar Bolling was a student at a small Lutheran college in Kansas. His religious convictions were strong even as a young man. He was known to carry a Bible around, and was sort of an unofficial preacher in his neighborhood back home. In the weeks after Pearl Harbor, he was prepared to set aside his study of the word of God to do his part for his country. In those days, young men of eighteen or nineteen years old— kids, really—were lining up to leave their homes, their families, their friends, to fight in a global conflict in which many, many people would die. At train stations across America, moms and dads said their good-byes to sons they might never hold again.

In that winter of 1942, Eric Bolling applied for naval aviation training. One of his professors at Bethany College wrote a letter of recommendation to the U.S. Navy, a letter that is now in my possession. The professor attested to young Eric's "fine character, high ideals, and tested loyalties which he will use in serving God in whatever opportunities and responsibilities given to him." I also have his Social Security card and a letter from the college registrar attesting that he was a student of good standing. These were documents Eric Bolling needed to enlist in the U.S. military.

Eric was accepted into naval aviation training, and was sent to the South Pacific. In July 1943, he, his entire crew, and their aircraft disappeared somewhere near the New Hebrides. For many years, that was where the trail went cold for me. That was all I knew. It was thanks to my work in television that I was eventually able to find out more.

A few years ago, when I mentioned my uncle's name during a segment on Fox News Channel, a viewer named Jim Wright—a Lutheran pastor in Texas, Air Force veteran, and World War II history buff—e-mailed me and said that he thought he had a picture of my uncle. He sent me a picture of a group of men in khaki uniforms in front of a World War II airplane. I immediately spotted a guy who looked a little like me at that age—with slicked-back hair and a determined look. The first Eric Bolling.

As it turned out, Jim Wright's uncle, Lloyd Richard Morgan of Tulsa, Oklahoma, and my uncle Eric from Chicago had served together on the same aircraft—they were both on it when it vanished. Wright had written a book about his uncle, my uncle, and the many other men who disappeared in the South Pacific entitled *The Search That Never Was*. Thanks to Wright's book, I was able to learn a lot more about Uncle Eric and the men he served with.[1]

Eric Bolling and Lloyd Morgan were the two aviation radiomen aboard a PB4Y-1 bomber, the Navy's version of the Army Air Corps' B-24 Liberator. They were part of the ten-man crew of a PB4Y-1 with the tail number 5V15, commanded by Lieutenant Junior Grade John Beverly Haskett. Their bomber squadron, VB-102, had had a busy spring of 1943 attacking Japanese warships and aircraft, according to Wright's research. They logged 990 sorties by April 30 of that year. On May 1, they arrived at a new base: Carney Airfield on Guadalcanal, an island in the Solomons chain that the United States had captured from the Japanese the previous year.

Wright's book notes that Lloyd Morgan, in a letter home to his family, referred to one of his crewmates, called "the Swede,"

as "apparently a preacher of some sort." Both Wright and I think
that he was talking about Eric Bolling—that deeply religious
young man of Swedish background who was a long way from
his Lutheran college.

In another letter, in March 1943, four months before he disappeared, young Lloyd asked his mother for a very specific kind
of care package. He asked for a .38-caliber handgun, ammuni-
tion, and a hunting knife. He didn't explain why he needed these
things, but it was known that the Japanese mistreated American personnel they had captured. Some were executed. It was
also not known if he ever had cause to use those weapons.

Jim Wright's book includes another picture showing radiomen Bolling and Morgan standing together with their comrades
in arms in front of a Liberator with *Galloping Ghost* painted on
the side. It's not known if that was the same plane they were on
when they went on their last mission.

Thanks to Wright's research, we do know that in the early
morning hours of Saturday, July 17, 1943, the PB4Y-1 carrying
Eric Bolling, Lloyd Morgan, and the rest of Lieutenant Junior
Grade Haskett's crew took off from Guadalcanal. Their aircraft,
with tail number 5V15, joined four other bombers to attack a
Japanese airfield on the island of Bougainville. They traveled
some 360 miles northward to reach their objective, and thanks
to the clear weather conditions were able to drop their 1,000-
pound cluster bombs mostly on target from about 11,000 feet.
The Japanese didn't even put up much antiaircraft fire. The whole
operation only took a few minutes.

Their bombing mission complete, the PB4Y-1s headed for
home. Just a few minutes out, at about 3:20 a.m., they came in
contact with a Japanese fighter aircraft. There is confusion as to
what happened next. Another Japanese fighter may have been
shot down. An American pilot reported two fireballs, one in
midair and another suggesting something had crashed into the
ocean below, near a Japanese-held island. Nobody heard a call
for "mayday," and nobody saw any parachutes, but while five

PB4Y-1 bombers had left Guadalcanal for the mission for Bougainville, only four returned. Eric Bolling's did not.

A month later, in August 1943, Lloyd Morgan's parents received a letter from the Department of the Navy informing them
that their twenty-year-old son had been reported missing in action. I can only imagine that my own grandparents received
one very similar. Again, it wasn't something Dad talked about.

"Words are of little help at such a time," the letter from Rear
Admiral D. C. Ramsey read, "but it is my fervent hope that
the knowledge of your son's loyalty to our country and his gal-
lant service in its defense will mitigate the bitterness of your
suffering."

No wreckage or any other trace of Bolling, Morgan, Haskett, or any of their crew or aircraft has ever been found.

As I've written this book, I've thought a lot about these young
men—my uncle, Lloyd Morgan, and thousands and thousands
like them. I also spent a lot of time thinking about many of the
nineteen- and twenty-year-olds we hear about in the news today.
They couldn't seem to be more different. Young people of Uncle
Eric's generation stepped up and became the soldiers, sailors, marines, airmen, and patriots that saved the world from fascism.
Today, our youth seem perfectly content to be socialists and
slackers. This isn't true of every young person. It isn't true of
my own son, for example. It's hard to deny, though, the perception that scores of idle and indulged permanent adolescents
have lost any sense of what made our country a great nation. I
know many of their parents and grandparents are aghast at what
has become of the generation who will, before long, lead this
nation. Right now they're running around demanding political correctness, seeking safe spaces, signing a petition—as they
did at Yale University not long ago—to repeal the First Amendment so they didn't have to hear opinions from people who
might offend them. Who knows, but I imagine a lot of them are
going to be up in arms about the tough love in this book, and its
lessons in outdated, uncool virtues like "manliness" and "thrift"

and "grit." It's something we hear and see all the time with our nation's brittle, sheltered youth—many of whom are too afraid to read a book without a trigger warning on the cover, let alone raise their hands and serve their nation in combat. I know many Americans are confused, frustrated, even angry about this, because I hear these things from viewers of my shows all the time. We've gone from the Greatest Generation to the Worst Generation in the span of seventy-five years.

I wrote *Wake Up America* to help us all fight back. To fight back against the forces of Left-wing, big-government zealots who seek to turn our country into a socialist utopia, where rules are handed down by pampered elites in Washington. To fight back against the damaging message being sent to our kids—that they are victims, that they need Daddy Government to bail them out and run their lives.

How do we fight this? By remembering what makes our country a truly exceptional place. By remembering the values and ideals that motivated countless young people like my Uncle Eric and his fellow crewmen to give their lives for a cause bigger than themselves. By reclaiming the things that made America great in the first place.

I love this country. I love it because it saved my life. It gave me the opportunities that allowed me to succeed based on my own drive and talents. It gave me second chances, and third chances. It allowed me to be anything I wanted to be—regardless of where I was born, or how much money I was worth, or who my parents were. I still believe *that* America exists, which is why I want to fight like hell to rescue it from people who don't understand what makes America the greatest nation on the face of the earth.

This book is organized around nine simple values that I believe truly define our nation, and separate us from nearly every other nation on earth. They can help us succeed as individuals—they've certainly helped me—and help America succeed as a nation. These values helped build the American character, and you can see it in every generation since our founding (at least, so far). They are:

- **Grit**: the power to try, fail, and rebuild in a nation of endless possibilities
- **Profit**: a system that rewards people for ingenuity, greed, and competition against others
- **Manliness**: the rugged pioneer spirit that allowed men and women with guts (and guns) to carve a great nation out of wilderness
- **Thrift**: the classic middle-American value of living within your means and avoiding debt
- **Individuality**: the ability to think and speak and believe whatever you like
- **Dominion**: the notion that nature is under the control of humanity, and not the other way around
- **Merit**: the idea that people should succeed based on their own skills and talents—not due to entitlements from a nanny state—and that effort and good choices should be rewarded
- **Pride**: love of country and an abiding belief in America's special place among the nations of the world
- **Providence**: the belief in a role for faith in our own lives and the life of our nation—from a simple ballgame to America's destiny—because there are things bigger than self or state

Even as I write this, the Left is at work to demonize every one of these qualities, in an effort to slowly take them away. Each of these American virtues poses an existential threat to the socialist paradise the Left wants to build in the land of the free. Which is why, as I have demonstrated, the Left is so intent on destroying them. It's why these virtues are deemed "trigger words" on college campuses, where shouting mobs of adolescent tin-pot despots shriek and complain about the "anguish" of capitalist, hetero-normative, and white-privileged American values.

It is time for all of us to wake up to a startling reality. The American dream is almost out the window, and it's making it all the more likely that a nightmare scenario is going to play out. If we're going to wake America up to this clear and present danger, and put a stop to it, these values are our best hope. The social engineers on the Left are winning. And they'll continue to, unless you, I, and millions of our fellow Americans raise our voices loud enough and stand up to stop them.

It is time for America to wake up to the looming arrival of a socialist state whose leaders are determined to rip away all the qualities and characteristics that have made us the most exceptional nation on earth. That's what this book is meant to do: to remind all of us of the values that made America the nation it is today. Values that shaped so many of our individual experiences. Values that in a very real way rescued me from poverty and saved my life.

NOTES

INTRODUCTION

1. www.realclearpolitics.com/articles/2008/10/obama_rallies_columbia_missour
   .html.
2. www.realclearpolitics.com/video/2015/07/30/chris_matthews_to_debbie
   _wasserman_schultz_whats_the_difference_between_a_democrat_and_a
   _socialist.html.
3. www.thedailybeast.com/articles/2015/11/04/bryan-cranston-s-first
   -amendment-crusade-on-trumbo-trump-and-why-he-respects-fox-news.html.

1. GRIT

1. www.cnn.com/2012/05/09/opinion/bennett-obama-campaign/index.html.
2. www.psychologytoday.com/articles/200411/nation-wimps.
3. www.theorrellgroup.com/2015/07/02/5-true-tales-of-gen-ys-parents-calling
   -bosses/.
4. www.ushistory.org/declaration/revwartimeline.html.
5. militaryhistory.about.com/od/americanrevolutio1/p/American-Revolution
   -General-George-Washington-A-Military-Profile.htm.
6. Ibid.
7. Ibid.
8. www.mountvernon.org/research-collections/digital-encyclopedia/article
   /valley-forge/.
9. Ibid.
10. www.econlib.org/library/Enc/bios/Smith.html.
11. www.econlib.org/library/Topics/Details/invisiblehand.html.
12. Ibid.
13. news.investors.com/ibd-editorials/073015-764333-tepid-gdp-growth-leaves
    -economy-even-further-behind-the-pace.htm.
14. Ibid.
15. www.usnews.com/news/the-report/articles/2015/07/16/unemployment-is
    -low-but-more-workers-are-leaving-the-workforce.
16. www.youtube.com/watch?v=banjkuLkW1M.
17. www.realclearpolitics.com/video/2011/09/29/president_obama_america_has
    _gone_soft.html.

2. PROFIT

1. www.huffingtonpost.com/2011/12/05/fox-news-the-muppets-are-communist_n_1129173.html.
2. www.motherjones.com/media/2011/12/muppets-fox-news.
3. www.theguardian.com/film/shortcuts/2011/dec/06/muppet-movies-communist-plots-revealed.
4. www.mediaite.com/tv/eric-bolling-trashes-environmental-message-of-the-muppets-the-evil-muppet-is-named-tex-richman/.
5. www.politico.com/story/2015/11/elizabeth-warren-tax-hike-deficit-216024#ixzz3uyVaxXd6.
6. corporate.walmart.com/_news_/walmart-facts/corporate-financial-fact-sheet.
7. www.archives.gov/exhibits/charters/virginia_declaration_of_rights.html.
8. John Locke, *Two Treatises of Government* (Awnsham Churchill, 1689).
9. www.economist.com/news/leaders/21578665-nearly-1-billion-people-have-been-taken-out-extreme-poverty-20-years-world-should-aim.
10. www.aei.org/publication/minimum-wage-effect-january-to-june-job-losses-for-seattle-area-restaurants-1300-largest-since-great-recession/.
11. Ibid.
12. www.investopedia.com/articles/economics/08/past-recessions.asp.
13. www.manhattan-institute.org/html/revisiting-high-tax-rates-1950s-5714.html.
14. www.aei.org/publication/returning-to-the-90-top-tax-rates-of-the-1950s-would-probably-be-terrible-for-the-us-economy/.
15. eml.berkeley.edu//~saez/piketty-saezJEP07taxprog.pdf.
16. www.nytimes.com/2015/12/02/technology/mark-zuckerberg-facebook-charity.html?_r=0.
17. Ibid.
18. medium.com/bull-market/mark-zuckerberg-s-45-billion-loophole-7dcff7b811b3#.fy5v7xqiy.
19. www.cbsnews.com/news/mark-zuckerberg-responds-to-critics-of-facebook-shares-donations/.
20. www.breitbart.com/big-hollywood/2014/07/23/michael-moore-owns-9-homes/.
21. linkis.com/la0UE.
22. www.youtube.com/watch?v=2aUADa_oWBA.
23. www.celebritynetworth.com/richest-celebrities/actors/matt-damon-net-worth/.
24. www.celebritynetworth.com/richest-celebrities/actors/meryl-streep-net-worth/.
25. work.chron.com/pay-scale-film-crew-1903.html.
26. www.washingtonpost.com/blogs/plum-line/wp/2015/05/26/bernie-sanders-calls-for-downward-transfer-of-wealth-of-top-one-percent/.
27. www.politifact.com/truth-o-meter/article/2015/oct/15/what-bernie-sanders-said-about-not-being-billionai/.
28. www.senate.gov/artandhistory/history/common/briefing/senate_salaries.htm.

29. www.deptofnumbers.com/income/us/.
30. money.cnn.com/2015/12/21/investing/hillary-clinton-wall-street-donations/.
31. www.nationalreview.com/article/219537/right-cares-interview.

3. MANLINESS

1. www.buzzfeed.com/emaoconnor/split-the-check-or-whatever#
   .qgQrRoqLN7.
2. Ibid.
3. www.news.com.au/lifestyle/relationships/chivalrous-behaviour-is-just-a
   -version-of-benevolent-sexism-study-says/news-story/ea9efe84c4a2c9a988405
   7098839629f.
4. www.inquisitr.com/1929611/major-shots-fired-in-mommy-war-being-a-stay
   -at-home-mom-is-a-hobby-not-a-job/.
5. www.washingtontimes.com/news/2015/jan/1/planned-parenthood-327k
   -abortions-fiscal-2014/.
6. Harvey Mansfield, *Manliness* (New Haven: Yale University Press, 2006), 23.
7. www.nytimes.com/2015/10/02/fashion/mens-style/27-ways-to-be-a-modern
   -man.html?_r=0.
8. www.huffingtonpost.com/entry/senator-claire-mccaskill-encourages-men-to
   -just-shut-the-hell-up_us_5642208ce4b0b24aee4be8ac.
9. www.csmonitor.com/USA/Politics/Decoder/2013/1218/Pajama-Boy-on
   -Obamacare-Will-Millennials-hear-a-grownup-in-a-onesie-video.
10. www.sandiego.edu/campus-life/detail.php?_focus=52641.
11. www.kmtv.com/news/local-news/unl-campaign-encourages-students-to
    -mind-their-manners.
12. www.breitbart.com/big-government/2014/04/26/duke-university-instructs
    -students-what-slang-they-can-t-use/.
13. abc7news.com/education/boy-suspended-over-imaginary-bow-and-arrow
    /1070526/.
14. www.washingtonpost.com/news/early-lead/wp/2016/01/10/donald-trump
    -nfl-football-has-become-soft-like-our-country-has-become-soft/.
15. www.nytimes.com/2015/02/05/opinion/nicholas-kristof-bruce-jenners
    -courage.html?_r=0.
16. www.nytimes.com/2015/02/05/opinion/gail-collins-american-sniper-moral
    .html.
17. salon.com/2016/01/27/camille_paglia_hillarys_blame_men_first_feminism
    _may_prove_costly_in_2016/.
18. www.telegraph.co.uk/women/womens-business/10306864/Women-feel-need
    -to-act-like-men-to-get-ahead-at-work.html.
19. www.vox.com/2015/3/26/8295285/nursing-pay-gap.
20. www.csmonitor.com/Business/2015/0609/Why-aren-t-there-more-female
    -mechanics-video.
21. www.thedailybeast.com/articles/2014/02/15/the-complete-glossary-of
    -facebook-s-51-gender-options.html.

22. www.cbsnews.com/news/uc-irvine-california-college-ask-students-pick-from
    -6-genders-in-application/.

23. www.nydailynews.com/news/politics/suny-policy-students-7-options
    -choosing-gender-article-1.2356382.

24. www.bostonglobe.com/metro/2015/09/02/harvard-allows-students-pick-new
    -gender-pronouns/C0EXpZHw09zwCzo4hVhjdJ/story.html.

25. Ibid.

4. THRIFT

1. www.hollywoodreporter.com/news/drunk-at-golden-globes-how-852119.

2. www.newsmax.com/FastFeatures/Barack-Obama-Solyndra-Scandal-Green
   -Energy/2015/01/29/id/621537/#ixzz3xoU3FuKv.

3. www.washingtontimes.com/news/2015/aug/26/solyndra-misled-government
   -get-535-million-solar-p/.

4. www.heritage.org/research/reports/2005/10/the-bridge-to-nowhere-a
   -national-embarrassment.

5. www.foxbusiness.com/features/2014/05/14/median-american-savings-0.html.

6. www.unc.edu/depts/diplomat/item/2007/0103/sich/sicherman_franklin.html.

7. www.thirteenvirtues.com/.

8. www.heritage.org/research/reports/2013/10/national-debt-and-the-founding
   -fathers.

9. Ibid.

10. www.newyorker.com/news/amy-davidson/how-much-money-does-bill
    -clinton-need.

11. www.forbes.com/sites/taxanalysts/2014/04/23/its-good-to-be-the-ex
    -president-but-it-wasnt-always/#2715e4857a0b670bd9f02d72.

12. Ibid.

13. Ibid.

14. Ibid.

15. www.people.com/people/archive/article/0,,20121579,00.html.

16. www.newyorker.com/news/amy-davidson/how-much-money-does-bill
    -clinton-need.

17. www.breitbart.com/big-government/2015/06/03/21-new-clinton-cash
    -revelations-that-have-imperiled-hillary-clintons-campaign/.

18. www.nytimes.com/2015/05/30/us/politics/an-award-for-bill-clinton-came
    -with-500000-for-his-foundation.html?_r=0.

19. www.ibtimes.com/clinton-foundation-donors-got-weapons-deals-hillary
    -clintons-state-department-1934187.

20. www.washingtonpost.com/politics/1100-donors-to-a-canadian-charity-tied
    -to-clinton-foundation-remain-secret/2015/04/28/c3c0f374-edbc-11e4-8666
    -a1d756d0218e_story.html.

21. www.vox.com/2015/4/28/8501643/Clinton-foundation-donors-State.

22. www.newyorker.com/news/amy-davidson/five-questions-about-the-clintons
    -and-a-uranium-company.

23. www.wsj.com/articles/gifts-to-hillary-clintons-family-charity-are
    -scrutinized-in-wake-of-book-1429754883.
24. www.nytimes.com/2015/04/24/us/cash-flowed-to-clinton-foundation-as
    -russians-pressed-for-control-of-uranium-company.html?_r=0.
25. www.nytimes.com/interactive/2015/04/23/us/clinton-foundation-donations
    -uranium-investors.html.
26. www.bloomberg.com/politics/articles/2015-04-25/author-alleges-bill-clinton
    -just-quit-education-company-because-of-clinton-cash-.
27. www.washingtonpost.com/politics/for-clintons-speech-income-shows-how
    -their-wealth-is-intertwined-with-charity/2015/04/22/12709ec0-dc8d-11e4
    -a500-1c5bb1d8ff6a_story.html.
28. www.politico.com/story/2015/04/moroccan-cash-flows-to-clinton
    -foundation-116780.
29. www.newyorker.com/news/amy-davidson/how-much-money-does-bill
    -clinton-need.
30. www.nytimes.com/2013/08/14/us/politics/unease-at-clinton-foundation
    -over-finances-and-ambitions.html.
31. Ibid.
32. www.newyorker.com/news/amy-davidson/how-much-money-does-bill
    -clinton-need.
33. dailysignal.com/2014/10/22/top-6-examples-wasteful-government-spending
    -wastebook-2014/.
34. Ted Cruz, *A Time for Truth: Reigniting The Promise of America* (New York:
    HarperCollins, 2015), x–xi.
35. www.cnbc.com/id/100700580.
36. www.nerdwallet.com/blog/credit-card-data/average-credit-card-debt
    -household/.
37. Ibid.
38. www.politico.com/story/2015/08/hillary-clintons-350-billion-plan-to-kill
    -college-debt-121210#ixzz3xz8dmCe2.
39. www.wsj.com/articles/price-tag-of-bernie-sanders-proposals-18-trillion
    -1442271511.
40. www.cbc.ca/news/business/google-to-refund-19m-us-for-kids-mobile
    -spending-sprees-1.2755769.
41. venturebeat.com/2014/01/15/apple-refund-32-million-parents-iap/.

5. INDIVIDUALITY

1. freebeacon.com/issues/government-bans-bacon-on-federal-prison-menus
   -adds-turkey-substitute/.
2. www.salon.com/2015/12/09/lets_have_a_war_on_football_greed_brain
   _damage_tax_breaks_to_billionaires_and_the_debate_we_need_to_have
   _about_the_nfl/.
3. michellemalkin.com/2008/11/04/fairness-doctrine-watch-schumer-likes
   -conservative-opinion-to-pornography/.

4. www.foxnews.com/us/2015/12/16/yale-fail-ivy-leaguers-caught-on-video
-clamoring-to-kill-first-amendment.html?intcmp=hpbt4.

5. ballotpedia.org/California_Proposition_8,_the_%22Eliminates_Right_of
_Same-Sex_Couples_to_Marry%22_Initiative_%282008%29.

6. msa.maryland.gov/msa/mdstatehouse/html/gwresignation.html.

7. archive.org/stream/TheBlackBookofCommunism10/the-black-book-of
-communism-jean-louis-margolin-1999-communism_djvu.txt.

8. www.congress.gov/bill/113th-congress/senate-joint-resolution/19?q
={%22search%22%3A[%22sjr+19%22.

9. www.breitbart.com/big-government/2014/05/18/harry-reid-vote-to-amend
-u-s-constitution-to-limit-political-speech/.

10. www.britannica.com/event/Enlightenment-European-history.

11. www.thedailybeast.com/articles/2015/11/16/brown-students-poisonous
-uprising-against-their-president.html.

12. www.thedailybeast.com/articles/2015/12/06/brown-university-professor
-denounces-mccarthy-witch-hunts.html.

13. www.wsj.com/news/articles/SB10001424052702303465004579322773368846
510.

14. www.mrc.org/media-bias-101/journalists-admitting-liberal-bias-part-one.

15. www.wsj.com/articles/SB10001424052702304680904579366903828260732;
dailycaller.com/2012/05/26/should-fox-news-be-banned/.

16. Those affiliated with CREW include prominent Hillary Clinton supporter
David Brock, along with others with a long history of working for liberal
Democrats.

6. DOMINION

1. www.gallup.com/poll/183275/say-animals-rights-people.aspx.

2. www.slate.com/blogs/wild_things/2013/12/26/pet_parent_or_pet_owner
_caring_for_cats_and_dogs_is_not_like_raising_children.html.

3. Ibid.

4. www.telegraph.co.uk/news/newstopics/howaboutthat/8479391/Calling
-animals-pets-is-insulting-academics-claim.html.

5. Ibid.

6. Ibid.

7. freegan.info/.

8. Ibid.

9. Ibid.

10. www.loc.gov/teachers/classroommaterials/presentationsandactivities
/presentations/timeline/colonial/jamestwn/founding.html.

11. appalachianmagazine.com/2015/02/01/the-rattlesnake-americas-first-national
-symbol/.

12. www.huffingtonpost.ca/douglas-anthony-cooper/peta-kill_b_1387030.html.

13. www.peta.org/about-peta/why-peta/why-animal-rights/.

14. www.peta.org/features/ingrid-newkirks-unique-will/.

15. Ibid.
16. John Hardwig, "Is There a Duty to Die?" Hastings Center Report 27, no. 2 (1997), 34–42.
17. books.google.com/books?id=6J20_fbVwhYC&pg=PT100&lpg=PT100&dq =david+graber+%22Became+a+cancer%22&source=bl&ots=baAY38N_b4 &sig=3xMwCuwiA77BB31rzUy2sL8aFJU&hl=en&sa=X&ved=0ahUKEwj6o 5yW38rKAhWKKh4KHYlIDpEQ6AEIIjAB#v=onepage&q=david%20 graber%20%22Became%20a%20cancer%22&f=false.
18. www.aim.org/wls/author/david-foreman/.
19. books.google.com/books?id=46OGAgAAQBAJ&pg=PA356&lpg=PA356&dq =foreman+reduce+human+population+100+million&source=bl&ots =FSva3CScMd&sig=JCnsuzds1rzoP5ycoXujgWVR0KY&hl=en&sa=X&ved= 0ahUKEwjMiuy31crKAhUBqB4KHfxwDPk4ChDoAQgbMAA#v=onepage &q=foreman%20reduce%20human%20population%20100%20million&f =false.
20. books.google.com/books?id=GF7tXZ6tz8EC&pg=PA128&lpg=PA128&dq =paul+watson+%22humans+are+superior%22&source=bl&ots=VnogPxdAv3 &sig=7wSRGr1KjhAbsRXTbywATsK_uF0&hl=en&sa=X&ved=0ahUKEwj T0sG61srKAhVFcj4KHcXUDQkQ6AEIKDAC#v=onepage&q=paul%20 watson%20%22humans%20are%20superior%22&f=false.
21. www.americanthinker.com/articles/2010/08/sustainable_poverty_the_real _f.html.
22. www.gallup.com/poll/183275/say-animals-rights-people.aspx.
23. www.peta.org/blog/mommy-kills-animals-take-2/.
24. www.petakillsanimals.com/wp-content/uploads/2014/06/mommykills.pdf.
25. www.consumerfreedom.com/press-releases/facing-legislative-blow-petas -animal-house-of-horrors-killed-88-percent-of-dogs-and-cats-in-its -possession-in-2014/.
26. www.huffingtonpost.com/2015/02/05/pets-shelter-euthanization-rate_n _6612490.html.
27. www.delmarvanow.com/story/news/local/virginia/2014/11/23/peta -accomack-protest/19446725/.
28. www.nydailynews.com/news/national/peta-steals-va-family-dog-kills-dad -article-1.2010408.
29. www.ktvb.com/story/news/crime/2015/07/25/animal-activists-release-mink -burley/30674845/.
30. Ibid.
31. Ibid.
32. www.theharrispoll.com/health-and-life/Pets_Really_Are_Members_of_the _Family.html.
33. www.newsweek.com/instagram-dogs-wedding-zolatoastsfinn-415805.
34. Ibid.
35. Ibid.
36. www.dailymail.co.uk/news/article-2861980/Hunter-gets-death-threats -killing-rare-albino-deer-posting-photos-Facebook.html.

37. Ibid.
38. www.scienceheroes.com/index.php?option=com_content&view=article&id=80&Itemid=115.
39. forestry.about.com/cs/treeplanting/a/tree_plt_stats.htm.
40. www.fao.org/docrep/meeting/x4995e.htm.

7. MERIT

1. worldnews.about.com/od/unitedstates/f/nobelprizeprez.htm.
2. en.wikipedia.org/wiki/2009_Nobel_Peace_Prize.
3. www.barackobama.com/president-obama/.
4. www.biography.com/people/barack-obama-12782369.
5. Ibid.
6. www.washingtonpost.com/wp-dyn/articles/A19751-2004Jul27.html.
7. www.biography.com/people/barack-obama-12782369.
8. www.nobelprize.org/nobel_prizes/peace/laureates/2009/.
9. www.whitehouse.gov/the-press-office/remarks-president-winning-nobel-peace-prize.
10. www.washingtontimes.com/news/2015/sep/16/nobel-panel-saw-obama-peace-prize-mistake-new-book/.
11. www.pbs.org/wgbh/americanexperience/features/primary-resources/reagan-farewell/.
12. reason.com/poll/2014/08/19/57-percent-of-americans-say-only-kids-wh.
13. Ibid.
14. www.businessinsider.com/rick-santelli-tea-party-rant-2014-2.
15. www.newsbusters.org/blogs/tom-blumer/2009/02/19/rant-ages-cnbcs-rick-santelli-goes-studio-hosts-invoke-mob-rule-downplay#sthash.pxeVru2W.dpuf.
16. Ibid.

8. PRIDE

1. www.hollywoodreporter.com/news/ariana-grande-says-i-hate-807275.
2. www.foxnews.com/story/2008/02/19/michelle-obama-takes-heat-for-saying-shersquos-lsquoproud-my-countryrsquo-for.html.
3. www.gallup.com/poll/183911/smaller-majority-extremely-proud-american.aspx.
4. www.newsmax.com/US/annenberg-know-branches-government/2014/09/18/id/595561/.
5. www.newsweek.com/how-ignorant-are-americans-66053.
6. www.washingtonexaminer.com/a-third-of-americans-cant-name-any-of-their-rights-in-the-first-amendment/article/2567671.
7. www.nbclosangeles.com/news/local/Study-Americans-Dont-Know-About-Much-About-History.html.
8. www.reason.com/poll/2014/08/19/65-of-americans-say-millennials-are-enti.

9. www.washingtontimes.com/news/2015/dec/11/millennials-want-to-send
   -ground-troops-to-fight-is/.
10. freebeacon.com/culture/hayes-part-of-embracing-soccer-is-accepting-the
    -fact-the-u-s-cannot-simply-assert-its-dominance/.
11. www.jfklibrary.org/JFK/JFK-in-History/The-Cold-War-in-Berlin.aspx.
12. www.realclearpolitics.com/video/2015/07/30/chris_matthews_to_debbie
    _wasserman_schultz_whats_the_difference_between_a_democrat_and_a
    _socialist.html.
13. latimesblogs.latimes.com/washington/2009/01/post.html.
14. thefederalist.com/2015/06/05/sorry-ron-fournier-obamas-idea-of-american
    -exceptionalism-is-still-unexceptional/.
15. www.nationalreview.com/corner/418674/majority-democrats-37-percent
    -republicans-want-repeal-first-amendment-charles-c-w.
16. freebeacon.com/national-security/obama-admin-accuses-israel-of-terrorism
    -as-more-jews-murdered/.
17. www.telegraph.co.uk/news/worldnews/barackobama/5101244/President
    -Barack-Obama-America-has-been-arrogant-and-dismissive-towards-Europe
    .html.
18. www.whitehouse.gov/the-press-office/remarks-president-cairo-university-6
    -04-09.
19. www.breitbart.com/national-security/2015/03/02/nearly-six-years-after
    -obamas-cairo-speech-middle-east-in-total-disarray/.
20. www.politifact.com/texas/article/2015/nov/30/barack-obama-hasnt-said
    -radical-islamic-terrorism/.
21. www.pewresearch.org/fact-tank/2015/12/07/muslims-and-islam-key
    -findings-in-the-u-s-and-around-the-world/.
22. www.newsmax.com/US/Chuck-Schumer-Senate-bill-hate/2015/03/25/id
    /634536/.
23. www.uschamber.com/immigration.
24. www.breitbart.com/big-government/2015/04/21/polls-american-opposition
    -to-mass-immigration-guilt-trips-at-all-time-high/.
25. Ibid.
26. Ibid.
27. www.newsmax.com/US/Chuck-Schumer-Senate-bill-hate/2015/03/25/id
    /634536/.
28. www.theatlantic.com/business/archive/2015/10/get-rid-borders-completely
    /409501/.
29. www.nytimes.com/2012/11/20/opinion/brooks-the-conservative-future
    .html?ref=davidbrooks&_r=3&.
30. www.theatlantic.com/business/archive/2015/10/get-rid-borders-completely
    /409501/.
31. abcnews.go.com/International/wireStory/sweden-introduces-border-checks
    -stem-migrant-flow-36076158.
32. www.telegraph.co.uk/news/worldnews/europe/germany/12085182/Cover-up
    -over-Cologne-sex-assaults-blamed-on-migration-sensitivities.html.

33. www.cnn.com/2016/01/25/europe/sweden-asylum-seeker-stabs-woman/.
34. www.nationalreview.com/article/429192/immigration-new-culture-war.
35. Ibid.
36. www.buzzfeed.com/jessicagarrison/all-you-americans-are-fired#
    .odReGmM77.
37. Ibid.
38. www.breitbart.com/big-government/2015/04/21/polls-american-opposition
    -to-mass-immigration-guilt-trips-at-all-time-high/.
39. www.foxnews.com/us/2015/09/16/crime-wave-elusive-data-shows
    -frightening-toll-illegal-immigrant-criminals.html.
40. Ibid.
41. thehill.com/blogs/pundits-blog/immigration/264667-3-immigration-issues
    -unresolved-in-2015.
42. millercenter.org/president/speeches/speech-3364.
43. www.pbs.org/wgbh/americanexperience/features/primary-resources/reagan
    -farewell/.

9. PROVIDENCE

1. www.pewforum.org/2012/12/18/global-religious-landscape-christians/.
2. www.cnn.com/2015/12/04/opinions/bergen-san-bernardino-terror-attack
   -explain/.
3. www.whitehouse.gov/the-press-office/2015/12/03/statement-president
   -shooting-san-bernardino-california.
4. www.nytimes.com/2015/12/06/us/in-wake-of-shootings-a-familiar-call-to
   -arms-drives-latest-jump-in-weapon-sales.html.
5. www.nydailynews.com/news/politics/gop-candidates-call-prayers-calf
   -massacre-article-1.2453261.
6. www.washingtontimes.com/news/2013/sep/24/vatican-court-head-no
   -communion-nancy-pelosi/.
7. www.marxists.org/archive/marx/works/1843/critique-hpr/intro.htm.
8. www.npr.org/2015/12/21/460281546/watch-obama-says-trump-exploiting
   -anger-fear-among-blue-collar-men.
9. time.com/3702584/gay-marriage-axelrod-obama/.
10. erlc.com/article/some-positive-benefits-churches-bring-to-communities.
11. Ibid.
12. www.archives.gov/exhibits/charters/constitution_transcript.html.
13. www.dailymail.co.uk/news/article-2685923/Shocking-moment-ISIS
    -militants-sledgehammers-Mosul-tomb-Prophet-Jonah-50-blindfolded
    -bodies-massacred-south-Baghdad.html.
14. www.taipeitimes.com/News/editorials/archives/2015/04/12/2003615716.
15. www.washingtontimes.com/news/2015/dec/21/no-war-on-christmas-in
    -many-communities-officials-/?page=all.
16. www.breitbart.com/big-government/2015/09/16/white-house-invites-trio
    -catholic-dissenters-greet-pope-francis/.

17. www.wsj.com/articles/vatican-disputes-white-house-guest-list-for-papal-visit
    -1442533549.
18. www.hrw.org/world-report/2015/country-chapters/china-and-tibet.
19. www.hrw.org/world-report/2015/country-chapters/china-and-tibet.
20. www.nytimes.com/2015/09/26/world/asia/xi-jinping-white-house.html.

9. EPILOGUE

1. J. L. Wright, *The Search That Never Was: The Untold Truth about the 1948–49
   Search for World War II American Personnel Missing in Action in the South Pacific*
   (Houston, TX: Strategic Book Publishing and Rights Co., 2014).

INDEX